An Autobiography

by
Catherine Helen Spence

CONTENTS

I.	EARLY LIFE IN SCOTLAND.
II.	TOWARDS AUSTRALIA.
III.	A BEGINNING AT SEVENTEEN
IV.	LOVERS AND FRIENDS.
V.	NOVELS AND A POLITICAL INSPIRATION.
VI.	A TRIP TO ENGLAND.
VII.	MELROSE REVISITED.
VIII.	I VISIT EDINBURGH AND LONDON.
IX.	MEETING WITH J. S. MILL AND GEORGE ELIOT.
X.	RETURN FROM THE OLD COUNTRY.
XI.	WARDS OF THE STATE.
XII.	PREACHING, FRIENDS, AND WRITING.
XIII.	MY WORK FOR EDUCATION.
XIV.	SPECULATION, CHARITY, AND A BOOK.
XV.	JOURNALISM AND POLITICS.
XVI.	SORROW AND CHANGE.
XVII.	IMPRESSIONS OF AMERICA.
XVIII.	BRITAIN, THE CONTINENT, AND HOME AGAIN.
XIX.	PROGRESS OF EFFECTIVE VOTING.
XX.	WIDENING INTERESTS.
XXI.	PROPORTIONAL REPRESENTATION AND FEDERATION.
XXII.	A VISIT TO NEW SOUTH WALES.
XXIII.	MORE PUBLIC WORK.
XXIV.	THE EIGHTIETH MILESTONE AND THE END.

CHAPTER I
EARLY LIFE IN SCOTLAND

Sitting down at the age of eighty-four to give an account of my life, I feel that it connects itself naturally with the growth and development of the province of South Australia, to which I came with my family in the year 1839, before it was quite three years old. But there is much truth in Wordsworth's line, "the child is father of the man," and no less is the mother of the woman; and I must go back to Scotland for the roots of my character and Ideals. I account myself well-born, for My father and my mother loved each other. I consider myself well descended, going back for many generations on both sides of intelligent and respectable people. I think I was well brought up, for my father and mother were of one mind regarding the care of the family. I count myself well educated, for the admirable woman at the head of the school which I attended from the age of four and a half till I was thirteen and a half, was a born teacher in advance of her own times. In fact. like my own dear mother, Sarah Phin was a New Woman without knowing it. The phrase was not known in the thirties.

I was born on October 31, 1825, the fifth of a family of eight born to David Spence and Helen Brodie, in the romantic village of Melrose, on the silvery Tweed, close to the three picturesque peaks of the Eildon Hills, which Michael Scott's familiar spirit split up from one mountain mass in a single night, according to the legend. It was indeed poetic ground. It was Sir Walter Scott's ground. Abbotsford was within two miles of Melrose, and one of my earliest recollections was seeing the long procession which followed his body to the family vault at Dryburgh Abbey. There was not a local note in "The Lay of the Last Minstrel" or in the novels. "The Monastery" and "The Abbot," with which I was not familiar before I entered my teens. There was not a hill or a burn or a glen that had not a song or a proverb, or a legend about it. Yarrow braes were not far off. The broom of the Cowdenknowes was still nearer, and my mother knew the words as well as the tunes of the minstrelsy of the

Scottish Border. But as all readers of the life of Scott know, he was a Tory, loving the past with loyal affection, and shrinking from any change. My father, who was a lawyer (a writer as it was called), and his father who was a country practitioner, were reformers, and so it happened that they never came into personal relations with the man they admired above all men in Scotland. It was the Tory doctor who attended to his health, and the Tory writer who was consulted about his affairs.

I look back to a happy childhood. The many anxieties which reached both my parents were quite unknown to the children till the crisis in 1839. I do not know that I appreciated the beauty of the village I lived in so much with my own bodily eyes as through the songs and the literature, which were current talk. The old Abbey, with its 'prentice window, and its wonders in stonecarving, that Scott had written about and Washington Irving marvelled at—"Here lies the race of the House of Yair" as a tombstone—had a grand roll in it. In the churchyard of the old Abbey my people on the Spence side lay buried. In the square or market place there no longer stood the great tree described in The Monastery as standing just after Flodden Field, where the flowers of the forest had been cut down by the English; but in the centre stood the cross with steps up to it, and close to the cross was the well, to which twice a day the maids went to draw water for the house until I was nine years old, when we had pipes and taps laid on. The cross was the place for any public speaking, and I recalled, when I was recovering from the measles, the maid in whose charge I was, wrapped me in a shawl and took me with her to hear a gentleman from Edinburgh speak in favour of reform to a crowd gathered round. He said that the Tories had found a new name—they called themselves Conservatives because it sounded better. For his part he thought conserves were pickles, and he hoped all the Tories would soon find themselves in a pretty pickle. There were such shouts of laughter that I saw this was a great joke.

We had gasworks in Melrose when I was 10 or 11, and a great joy to us children the wonderful light was. I recollect the first lucifer matches, and the wonder of them. My brother John had got 6d. from a visiting, uncle as a reward for buying him snuff to fill his cousin's silver snuffbox, and he spent the money in buying a box of lucifers, with the piece of sandpaper doubled, through which each match was to be smartly drawn, and he took all of us and some of his friends to the orchard, we called the wilderness, at the back of my grandfather Spence's house, and lighted each of the 50 matches, and we considered it a great exhibition. 'MY grandfather (old Dr. Spence) died before the era of lucifer matches. He used to get up early and strike a fire with flint and steel to boil the kettle and make a cup of tea to give to his wife in bed. He did it for his first wife (Janet Park), who was delicate, and he did the same for his second wife until her last fatal illness. It was a wonderful thing for a man to do in those days. He would not call the maid; he said young things wanted plenty of sleep. He had been a navy doctor, and was very intelligent. He trusted much to Nature and not too much to drugs. On the Sunday of the great annular eclipse of the sun in 1835, which was my brother John's eleventh birthday, he had a large double tooth extracted—not by a dentist, and gas was then unknown or any other anaesthetic, so he did not enjoy the eclipse as other people did. It took place in the afternoon, and there was no afternoon church.

In summer we had two services—one in the forenoon and one in the afternoon. In winter we had two services at one sitting, which was a thing astonishing to English visitors. The first was generally called a lecture—a reading with comments, of a passage of Scripture—a dozen verses or more—and the second a regularly built sermon, with three or four heads, and some particulars, and a practical summing up.

Prices and cost of living had fallen since my mother had married in 1815, three months after the battle of Waterloo. At that time tea cost 8/0 a lb., loaf sugar, 1/4, and brown sugar 11 1/2d. Bread and meat were then still at war prices, and calico was no cheaper than linen, and that was dear. She paid 3/6 a yard for fine calico to make petticoats. Other garments were of what was called home made linen. White cotton stockings at 4/9, and thinner at 3/9 each; silk stockings at 11/6. I know she paid 36/ for a yard of

Brussels net to make caps of. It was a new thing to have net made in the loom. When a woman married she must wear caps at least in the morning. In 1838 my mother bought a chest of tea (84 lb.) for 20 pounds, a trifle under 5/0 a lb.; the retail price was 6/0—it was a great saving; and up to the time of our departure brown sugar cost 7 1/2d., and loaf sugar 10d. It is no wonder that these things were accounted luxuries. When a decent Scotch couple in South Australia went out to a station in the country in the forties and received their stores, the wife sat down at her quarter-chest of tea and gazed at her bag of sugar, and fairly wept to think of her old mother across the ocean, who had such difficulty in buying an ounce of tea and a pound of sugar. My mother even saw an old woman buy 1/4oz. of tea and pay 1 1/2d. for it, and another woman buy 1/4lb. of meat.

We kept three maids. The cook got 8 pounds a year, the housemaid 7 pounds, and the nursemaid 6 pounds, paid half-yearly, but the summer half-year was much better paid than the winter, because there was the outwork in the fields, weeding and hoeing turnips and potatoes, and haymaking. The winter work in the house was heavier on account of the fires and the grate cleaning, but the wages were less. My mother gave the top wages in the district, and was considerate to her maids, but I blush yet to think how poorly those good women who made the comfort of my early home were paid for their labours. You could get a washerwoman for a shilling or 1/6 a day, but you must give her a glass of whisky as well as her food. You could get a sewing girl for a shilling or less, without the whisky. And yet cheap as sewing was it was the pride of the middle-elms women of those days that they did it all themselves at home. Half of the time of girls' schools was given to sewing when mother was taught. Nearly two hours a day was devoted to it in my time.

A glass of whisky in Scotland in the thirties cost less than a cup of tea. I recollect my father getting a large cask of whisky direct from the distillery which cost 6/6 a gallon, duty paid. A bottle of inferior whisky could be bought at the grocer's for a shilling. It is surprising how much alcoholic beverages entered into the daily life, the business, and the pleasures of the people in those days. No bargain could be made without them. Christenings, weddings, funerals—all called for the pouring out of strong drink. If a lady called, the port and sherry decanters were produced, and the cake basket. If a gentleman, probably it was the spirit decanter. After the 3 o'clock dinner there was whisky and hot water and sugar, and generally the came after the 10 o'clock supper. Drinking habits were very prevalent among men, and were not in any way disgraceful, unless excessive. But there was less drinking among women than there is now, because public opinion was strongly against it. Without being abstainers, they were temperate. With the same heredity and the same environment, you would see all the brothers pretty hard drinkers and all the sisters quite straight. Such is the effect of public opinion. Nothing else has been so powerful in changing these customs as the cheapening of tea and coffee and cocoa, but especially tea.

My brothers went to the parish school, one of the best in the county. The endowment from the tiends or tithes, extorted by John Knox from the Lords of the congregations, who had seized on the church lands, was more meagre for the schoolmasters than for the clergy. I think Mr. Thomas Murray had only 33 pounds in Money, a schoolhouse, and a residence and garden, and he had to make up a livelihood from school fees, which began at 2/ a quarter for reading, 3/6 when writing was taught, and 5I for arithmetic. Latin, I think, cost 10/6 a quarter, but it included English. Mr. Murray adopted a phonic system of teaching reading, not so complete as the late Mr. Hartley formulated for our South Australian schools, and was most successful with it. He not only used maps, but he had blank maps-a great innovation. My mother was only taught geography during the years in which she was "finished" in Edinburgh, and never saw a map then. She felt interested in geography when her children were learning it. No boy in Mr. Murray's school was allowed to be idle; every spare minute was given to arithmetic. In the parish school boys of all classes were taught. Sir David Brewster's sons went to it; but there were fewer girls, partly because no needlework was taught there, and needlework was of supreme importance. Mr. Murray was session clerk, for which he received 5 pounds a year. On Saturday afternoons he might do land measuring, like Goldsmith's schoolmaster in "The Deserted Village"—

Lands he could measure, terms and tides presage,

And even the rumour ran that he could gauge.

My mother felt that her children were receiving a much better education than she had had. The education seemed to begin after she left school. Her father united with six other tenant farmers in buying the third edition of "The Encyclopedia Britannica," seven for the price of six. Probably it was only in East Lothian that seven such purchasers could be found, and my mother studied it well, as also the unabridged Johnson's Dictionary in two volumes. She learned the Greek letters, so that she could read the derivations, but went no further. She saw the fallacy of Mr. Pitt's sinking fund when her father believed in it. To borrow more than was needed so as to put aside part on compound interest, would make the price of money rise. And why should not private people adopt the same way of getting rid of debts? The father said it would not do for them at all—it was only practicable for a nation. The things I recollect of the life in the village of Melrose, of 700 inhabitants, have been talked over with my mother, and many embodied in a little MS. volume of reminiscences of her life. I hold more from her than from my father; but, as he was an unlucky speculator, I inherit from him Hope, which is invaluable to a social or political reformer. School holidays were only a rarity in harvest time for the parish school. At Miss Phin's we had, besides, a week at Christmas. The boys had only New Year's Day. Saturday was only a half-holiday. We all had a holiday for Queen Victoria's coronation, and I went with a number of school fellows to see Abbotsford, not for the first time in my life.

Two mail coaches—the Blucher and the Chevy Chase—ran through Melrose every day. People went to the post office for their letters, and paid for them on delivery. My two elder sisters—Agnes, who died of consumption at the age of 16, and Jessie, afterwards Mrs. Andrew Murray, of Adelaide and Melbourne, went to boarding school with their aunt, Mary Spence, lit Upper

Wooden, halfway between Jedburgh and Kelso. Roxburghshire is rich in old monasteries. The border lands were more safe in the hands of the church than under feudal lords engaged in perpetual fighting, and the vassals of the abbeys had generally speaking, a more secure existence. Kelso. Jedburgh, and Dryburgh Abbeys lay in fertile districts, and I fancy that when these came into the hands of the Lords of the congregation, the vassals looked back with regret on the old times. I was not sent to Wooden, but kept at home, and I went to a dayschool called by the very popish name of St. Mary's Convent, though it was quite sufficiently Protestant. My mother had the greatest confidence in the lady who was at the head of it. She had been a governess in good situations, and had taught herself Latin, so that she might fit the boys of the family to take a good place in the Edinburgh High School. She discovered that she had an incurable disease, a form of dropsy, which compelled her to lie down for some time every day, and this she considered she could not do as a governess. So she determined to risk her savings, and start a boarding and day school in Melrose, a beautiful and healthy neighbourhood, and with the aid of a governess, impart what was then considered the education of a gentlewoman to the girls in the neighbourhood. She took with her her old mother, and a sister who managed the housekeeping, and taught the pupils all kinds of plain and fancy needlework. She succeeded, and she lived till the year 1866, although most of her teaching was done from her sofa. When my mother was asked what it was that made Phin so successful, and so esteemed, she said it was her commonsense. The governesses were well enough, but the invalid old lady was the life and soul of the school. There were about 14 boarders, and nearly as many day scholars there, so long as there was no competition. When that came there was a falling off, but my young sister Mary and I were faithful till the day when after nine years at the same school, I went with Jessie to Wooden, to Aunt Mary's, to hear there that my father was ruined, and had to leave Melrose and Scotland for ever, and that we must all go to Australia. That was in April, 1839.

As I said, I had a very happy childhood. The death of my eldest sister at 16, and of my youngest sister at two years old, did not sink into the mind of a child as it did into that of my parents, and although they were seriously alarmed about my health when I was 12 years old, when I developed symptoms similar to those of Agnes at the same age, I was not ill enough to get at all alarmed. I was annoyed at having to stay away from school for three months. When the collapse came Jessie had a dear friend of some years' standing, and I had one whom had known only for some months, but I had spent a month with her in Edinburgh at Christmas, 1838, and we exchanged letters weekly through the box which came from Edinburgh with my brother John's, washing. It was too expensive for us to write by the post. Well, neither of our friends wrote a word to us. With regard to mine it was not to be wondered at much—she was only 13—but the other was more surprising. It was not till 1865 that an old woman told me that when Miss F. B. came to return some books and music to her to give to my aunt in Melrose, "she just sat in the chair and cried as if her heart would break." She was not quite a free agent. Very few single women were free agents in 1839. We were hopelessly ruined, our place would know us no more.

The only long holidays I had in the year I spent at Thornton Loch, in East Lothian, 40 miles away. I did not know that my father was a heavy speculator in foreign wheat, and I thought his keen interest in the market in Mark lane was on account of the Thornton Loch crops, in which first my grandfather and afterwards the three Maiden aunts were deeply concerned. My mother's father, John Brodie, was one of the most enterprising agriculturists in the most advanced district of Great Britain. He won a prize of two silver salvers from the Highland Society for having the largest area of drilled wheat sown. He was called up twice to London to give evidence before Parliamentary committees on the corn laws, and he naturally approved of them, because, with three large farms held on 19 years' leases at war prices, the influx of cheap wheat from abroad would mean ruin. He proved that he paid 6,000 pounds a year for these three farms—two he worked himself, the third was for his eldest son; but he was liable for the rent. On his first London trip, my aunt Margaret accompanied him, and on his second he took my mother. That was in the year 1814, and both of them noted from the postchaise that farming was not up to what was done in East Lothian.

My grandfather Brodie was a speculating man, and he lost nearly all his savings through starting, along with others, an East Lothian Bank, because the local banker had been ill used by the British Linen Company. He put in only 1,000 pounds; but was liable for all, and, as many of his fellow shareholders were defaulters, it cost 15,000 pounds before all was over, and if it had not been that he left the farm in the capable hands of Aunt Margaret, there would have been little or nothing left for the family. When he had a stroke of paralysis he wanted to turn over Thornton Loch, the only farm he then had, to his eldest son, but there were three daughters, and one of them said she would like to carry it on, and she did so. She was the most successful farmer in the country for 30 years, and then she transferred it to a nephew. The capacity for business of my Aunt Margaret, the wit and charm of my brilliant Aunt Mary, and the sound judgment and accurate memory of my own dear mother, showed me early that women were fit to share in the work of this world, and that to make the world pleasant for men was not their only mission. My father's sister Mary was also a remarkable and saintly woman, though I do not think she was such a born teacher as Miss Phin. When my father was a little boy, not 12 years old, an uncle from Jamaica came home for a visit. He saw his sister Janet a dying woman, with a number of delicate-looking children, and he offered to take David with him and treat him like his own son. No objections were made. The uncle was supposed to be well-to-do, and he was unmarried, but he took fever and died, and was found to be not rich but insolvent. The boy could read and write, and he got something to do on a plantation till his father sent money to pay his passage home. He must have been supposed to be worth something, for he got a cask of rum for his wages, which was shipped home, and when the duty had been paid was drunk in the doctor's household. But the boy had been away only 21 months, and he returned to find his mother dead, and two or three little brothers and sisters dead and buried, and his father married again to his mother's cousin, Katherine Swanston, an old maid of 45, who, however, two years afterwards was the mother of a fine big daughter, so that Aunt Helen Park's scheme for getting the money for her sister's children failed. In spite of my father's strong wish to be a farmer, and not a writer or attorney, there was no capital to start a farm upon, so he was indentured to Mr. Erskine, and after some years began business in Melrose for himself, and married Lelen (Helen?) Brodie. His elder brother John went as a surgeon in the Royal Navy—before he was twenty-one. The demand for surgeons was great during the war time. He was made a Freemason before the set age, because in case of capture friends from the fraternity might be of great use. He did not like his original profession, especially when after the peace he must be a country practitioner like his father, at every one's beck and call, so he was articled to his brother, and lived in the house till he married and settled at Earlston, five miles off. Uncle John Spence was a scholarly man, shy but kindly, who gave to us children most of the books we possessed. They were not in such abundance as children read nowadays, but they were read and re-read.

In these early readings the Calvinistic teaching of the church and the shorter catechism was supported and exemplified. The only secular books to counteract them were the "Evenings at Home" and Miss Edgeworth's "Tales for Young and Old!" The only cloud on my young life was the gloomy religion, which made me doubt of my own salvation and despair of the salvation of any but a very small proportion of the people in the world. Thus the character of God appeared unlovely, and it was wicked not to love God; and this was my condemnation. I had learned the shorter catechism with the proofs from Scripture, and I understood the meaning of the dogmatic theology. Watts's hymns were much more easy to learn, but the doctrine was the same. There was no getting away from the feeling that the world was under a curse ever since that unlucky appleeating in the garden of Eden. Why, oh! why had not the sentence of death been carried out at once, and a new start made with more prudent people? The school in which as a day scholar I passed nine years of my life was more literary than many which were more pretentious. Needlework was of supreme importance, certainly, but during the hour and a half every day, Saturday's half-holiday not excepted, which was given to it by the whole school at once (odd half-hours were also put in), the best readers took turns about to read some book selected by Miss Phin. We were thus trained to pay attention. History, biography, adventures, descriptions, and story books were read. Any questions or criticisms about our sewing, knitting, netting, &c., were carried on in a low voice, and we learned to work well and quickly, and good reading aloud was cultivated. First one brother and then another had gone to Edinburgh for higher education than could be had at Melrose Parish School, and I wanted to go to a certain institution, the first of the kind, for advanced teaching for girls, which had a high reputation. I was a very ambitious girl at 13. I wanted to be a teacher first, and a great writer afterwards. The qualifications for a teacher would help me to rise to literary fame, so I obtained from my father a promise that I should go to Edinburgh next year; but he could not keep it. He was a ruined man.

CHAPTER II
TOWARDS AUSTRALIA

Although my mother's family had lost heavily by him, her mother gave us 500 pounds to make a start in South Australia. An 80-acre section was built for 80 pounds, and this entitled us to the steerage passage of four adults. This helped for my elder sister and two brothers (my younger brother David was left for his education with his aunts in Scotland), but we had to have another female, so we took with us a servant girl—most ridiculous, it seems now. I was under the statutory age of 15. The difference between steerage and intermediate fares had to be made up, and we sailed from Greenock in July, 1839, in the barque Palmyra, 400 tons, bound for Adelaide, Port Phillip, and Sydney. The Palmyra was advertised to carry a cow and an experienced surgeon. Intermediate passengers had no more advantage of the cow than steerage folks, and except for the privacy of separate cabins and a pound of white biscuit per family weekly, we fared exactly as the other immigrants did, though the cost was double. Twice a week we had either fresh meat or tinned meat, generally soup and boudle, and the biscuit seemed half bran, and sometimes it was mouldy. But our mother thought it was very good for us to endure hardship, and so it was.

There were 150 passengers, mostly South Australian immigrants, in the little ship. The first and second class passengers were bound for Port Philip and Sydney in greater proportion than for Adelaide There was in the saloon the youthful William Milne, and in the intermediate was Miss Disher, his future wife. He became President of the Legislative Council, and was knighted. There was my brother, J. B. Spence, who also sat in the Council, and was at one time Chief Secretary. There was George Melrose, a successful South Australian pastoralist; there was my father's valued clerk, Thomas Laidlaw, who was long in the Legislative Council of New South Wales and the leading man in the town of Yass. "Honest Torn of Yass" was his soubriquet. Bound for Melbourne there were Mr. and Mrs. Duncan, of Melrose, and

Charles Williamson, from Hawick, who founded a great business house in Collins Street. There were Langs from Selkirk, and McHaffies, who became pastoralists. Our next cabin mate, who brought out a horse, had the Richmond punt when there was no bridge there. All the young men were reading a thick book brought out by the Society for Promoting Useful Knowledge about sheep, but they could dance in the evenings to the strains of Mr. Duncan's violin, and although I was not 14, I was in request as a partner, as ladies were scarce. Jessie Spence and Eliza Disher, who were grown up, were the belles of the Palmyra. Of all the passengers in the ship the young doctor, John Logan Campbell, has had the most distinguished career. Next to Sir George Grey he has had most to do with the development of New Zealand. He is now called the Grand Old Man of Auckland. He had his twenty-first birthday, this experienced surgeon(!) in the same week as I had my fourteenth, while the Palmyra was lying off Holdfast Bay (now Glenelg) before we could get to the old Port Adelaide to discharge. My brother saw him in 1883, but I have not set eye on him since that week in 1839. We have corresponded frequently since my brother's death. In his book "Poenama," written for his children, there is a picture of the Palmyra, with an account of the voyage and the only sensational incident in it. We had a collision in the Irish Sea, and our foremast was broken, so that we had to return to Greenock for repairs, and then obtained the concession of white biscuit for the second class for one day in the week. Sir John Campbell's gift of a beautiful park to the citizens of Auckland was made while my brother John was alive. Just recently he has given money and plans for building and equipping the first free kindergarten in Auckland—perhaps in New Zealand—and as this includes a training college for the students it is very complete. These Palmyra passengers have made their mark on the history of Australia and New Zealand. It is surprising what a fine class of people immigrated to Australia in these days to face all the troubles of a new country.

The first issue of The Register was printed in London, and gave a glowing account of the province that was to be—its climate, its resources, the sound principles on which it was founded. It is sometimes counted as a reproach that South

Australia was founded by doctrinaires and that we retain traces of our origin; to me it is our glory. In the land laws and the immigration laws it struck out a new path, and sought to found a new community where the sexes should be equal, and where land, labour, and capital should work harmoniously together. Land was not to be given away in huge grants, as had been done in New South Wales and Western Australia, to people with influence or position, but was to be sold at the high price of 20/ an acre. The price should be not too high to bring out people to work on the land. The Western Australian settlers had been wellnigh starved, because there was no labour to give real value to the paper or parchment deeds. The cheapest fare third class was from 17 pounds to 20 pounds, and the family immigration, which is the best, was quite out of the reach of those who were needed. The immigrants were not bound to work for any special individual or company, unless by special contract voluntarily made. They were often in better circumstances after the lapse of a few years than the landbuyers, and, in the old days, the owner of an 80-acre section worked harder and for longer hours than any hired man would do, or could be expected to do.

In the South Australian Public Library there is a curious record—the minutes and proceedings of the South Australian Literary Society, in the years 1831-5. As the province was non-existent at that time, this cultivation of literature seems premature, but the members, 40 in number, were its founders, and pending the passage of the Bill by the Imperial Parliament, they met fortnightly in London to discuss its prospects, and to read papers on exploration and on matters of future development and government. The first paper was on education for the new land, and was read by Richard Davies Hanson. The South Australian Company and Mr. George Fife Angas came to the rescue by buying a considerable area of land and making up the amount of capital which was required. It is interesting to note that the casting vote in the House of Lords which decided that the province of South Australia should come into existence was given by the Duke of Wellington. Adelaide was to have been called Wellington, but somehow the Queen Consort's name carried the day. The name of the conquerer of Waterloo is immortalized in the capital of the Dominion of New Zealand, in the North Island, which, like South Australia, was founded on the Wakefield principle of selling land for money to be applied for immigration. The 40 signatures in the records of the South Australian Literary Society are most interesting to an old colonist like myself, and the names of many of them are perpetuated in those of our rivers and our streets:—Torrens, Wright, Brown, Gilbert, Gouger, Hanson, Kingston, Wakefield, Morphett, Childers, Hill (Rowland), Stephens, Mawn, Furniss, Symonds. The second issue of The Register was printed in Adelaide. It was also The Government Gazette. It gave the proclamation of the province, which was made under the historic gum tree near Holdfast Bay, now Glenelg. It also records the sales of the town acres which had not been allotted to the purchasers of preliminary sections. These were of 134 acres, and a town acre, at the price of 12/6 an acre. This was a temptation to invest at the very first, because afterwards the price was 20/ an acre, without any city lot. From this cheap investment came the frequent lamentation, "Why did not I buy Waterhouse's corner for 12/6?" But there was more than 12/6 needed. The investment was of 80 pounds, which secured the ownership of the corner block facing King William street and Rundle street, and besides 134 acres of valuable suburban land.

There were connected with The Register from the earliest days the enterprising head of the house. Robert Thomas, who must have been well aided by his intelligent wife. The sons and daughters took their place in colonial society. Mr. George Stevenson left the staff of The Globe and Traveller, a good old London Paper, to try his fortunes in the new Province founded on the Wakefield principle, as Private Secretary to the first Governor (Capt. John Hindmarsh, R.N.). It is matter of history how the Governor and the Commissioner of Lands differed and quarrelled, the latter having the money and the former the power of government, and it was soon found that Mr. Stevenson could wield a trenchant pen. He had been on the "Traveller" branch of the London paper what would be called now a travelling correspondent. The Governor was replaced by Col. Gawler, and Mr. Stevenson went on The Register as editor. Mrs. Stevenson was a clever woman, and could help her husband. She knew

Charles Dickens, and still better, the family of Hogarth, into which he married. My father and mother were surprised to find so good a paper and so well printed in the infant city. Then there were A. H. Davis, of the Reedbeds, and Nathaniel Hailes, who wrote under the cognomen of "Timothy Short," who had been publisher and bookseller. There was first Samuel Stephens, who came out in the first ship for the South Australian Company, and married a fellow passenger, Charlotte Hudson Beare, and died two years after, and then Edward, manager of the South Australian Bank, and later, John Stephens who founded The Weekly Observer, and afterwards bought The Register. These all belonged to a literary family.

People came out on the smallest of salaries with big families—H. T. H. Beare on 100 pounds a year as architect, for the South Australian Company, and he had 18 children by two wives. I do not know what salary Mr. William Giles came out on with nine children and a young second wife, but I am sure it was less than 300 pounds. His family in all counted 21. But things were bad in the old country before the great lift given by railways, and freetrade, which made England the carrier for the world; and the possibilities of the new country were shown in that first issue of The Register in London in the highest colours. Not too high by any means in the light of what has been accomplished in 73 years, but there was a long row to hoe first, and few of the pioneers reaped the prizes. But, in spite of hardships and poverty and struggle, the early colonial life was interesting, and perhaps no city of its size at the time contained as large a population of intelligent and educated people as Adelaide.

Mrs. Oliphant, writing in 1885 at the age of 57, says that reading the "Life of George Eliot" made her think of an autobiography, and this was written at the saddest crisis of her life. She survived her husband and all her children, and had just lost the youngest, the posthumous boy. For them and for the family of a brother she had carried on the strenuous literary work—fiction, biography, criticism, and history—and when she died at the age of 69 she had not completed the history of a great publishing house—that of Blackwood. Her life tallies with mine on many points, but it is not till I have completed my 84 years that her sad narrative impels me to set down what appears noteworthy in a life which was begun in similar circumstances, but which was spent mainly in Australia. The loss of memory which I see in many who are younger than myself makes me feel that while I can recollect I should fix the events and the ideals of my life by pen and ink. Like Mrs. Oliphant, I was born (three years earlier) in the south of Scotland. Like her I had an admirable mother but she lost hers at the age of 60, while I kept mine till she was nearly 97. Like Mrs. Oliphant, I was captivated by the stand made by the Free Church as a protest against patronage, and like her I shook off the shackles of the narrow Calvinism of Presbyterianism, and emerged into more light and liberty. But unlike Mrs. Oliphant, I have from my earliest youth taken an interest in politics, and although I have not written the tenth part of what she has done, I have within the last 20 years addressed many audiences in Australia and America, and have preached over 100 sermons. My personal influence has been exercised through the voice more strongly than by the pen, and in the growth and development of South Australia, to which I came with my parents and brothers and sisters when I was just 14, and the province not three years old, there have been opportunities for usefulness which might not have offered if I had remained in Melrose, in Sir Walter Scott's country.

CHAPTER III
A BEGINNING AT SEVENTEEN

    Perhaps my turn for economics was partly inherited from my mother, and emphasized by my father having been an unlucky speculator in foreign wheat, tempted thereto by the sliding scale, which varied from 33/ a quarter, when wheat was as cheap as it was in 1837, to 1/ a quarter, when it was 70/ in 1839. It was supposed that my father had made his fortune when he took his wheat out of bond but losses and deterioration during seven years, and interest on borrowed money—credit having been strained to the utmost—brought ruin and insolvency, and he had to go to South Australia, followed by his wife and family soon after. It seems strange that this disaster should be the culmination of the peace, after the long Napoleonic war. When my father married in 1815 he showed he was making 600 pounds a year, with 2,000 pounds book debts, as a writer or attorney and as agent for a bank. But the business fell off, the book debts could not be collected; the bank called up the advances; and for 24 years there was a struggle. My mother would not have her dowry of 1,500 pounds and other money left by an aunt settled on herself—neither her father nor herself approved of it—the wife's fortune should come and go with her husband's. My father first speculated in hops and lost heavily. He took up unlucky people, whom other business men had drained. I suppose he caught at straws. He had the gentlest of manners—"the politest man in Melrose," the old shoemaker called him. My paternal grandfather was Dr. William Spence, of Melrose. His father was minister of the Established Church at Cockburn's Path, Berwickshire. His grandfather was a small landed proprietor, but he had to sell Spence's mains, and the name was changed to Chirnside. So (as my father used to say) he was sprung from the tail of the gentry; while my mother was descended from the head of the commonalty. The Brodies had been tenant farmers in East Lothian for six or seven generations, though they originally came from the north. My grandfather Brodie thought abrogation of the Corn Laws meant ruin for the farmers, who had taken 19 years' leases at war prices. But during the war times both landlords and farmers coined money, while the labourers had high prices for food and very little increase in their wages. I recollect both grandfathers well, and through the accurate memory of my mother t can tell how middle-class people in lowland Scotland lived and dressed and travelled, entertained visitors, and worshipped God. She told me of the "dear years" 1799 and 1800, and what a terrible thing a bad crop was, when the foreign ports were closed by Napoleon. She told me that but for the shortlived Peace of Amiens she never heard of anything but war till the Battle of Waterloo settled it three months before her marriage. From her own intimate relations with her grandmother, Margaret Fernie Brodie, who was born in 1736, and died in 1817, she knew how two generations before her people lived and thought. So that I have a grasp on the past which many might envy, and yet the present and the future are even more to me, as they were to my mother. On her death in 1887 I wrote a quatrain for her memorial, and which those who knew her considered appropriate—

>HELEN BRODIE SPENCE
>
>Born at Whittingham, Scotland, 1791.
>
>Died at College Town, Adelaide, South Australia, 1887.
>
>Half a long life 'mid Scotland's heaths and pines,
>
>And half among our South Australian vines;
>
>Though loving reverence bound her to the past,
>
>Eager for truth and progress to the last.

Although my mother had the greatest love for Sir Walter Scott, and the highest appreciation of his poems and novels, she never liked Melrose. She liked Australia better after a while. Indeed, when we arrived in November, 1839, to a country so hot, so dry, so new, we felt like the good old founder of The Adelaide Register, Robert Thomas, when he came to the land described in his own paper as "flowing with milk and honey." Dropped anchor at Holdfast Bay. "When I saw the place at which we were to land I felt inclined to go and cut my throat." When we sat down on a log in Light square, waiting till my father brought the key of the wooden house In Gilles street, in spite of the dignity of my 14 years just attained, I had a good cry. There had been such a drought that they had a dearth, almost a famine. People like ourselves with 80 acre land orders were frightened to attempt cultivation in an unknown climate, with seed wheat at 25/ a bushel or more, and stuck to the town. We lived a month in Gilles street, then we bought a large marquee, and pitched it on Brownhill Creek, above where Mitcham now stands, bought 15 cows and a pony and cart, and sold the milk in town at 1/ a quart. But how little milk the cows gave in those days! After seven months' encamping, in which the family lived chiefly on rice—the only cheap food, of which we bought a ton—we came with our herd to West terrace, Adelaide. My father got the position of Town Clerk at 150 pounds a year twelve months after our arrival, and kept it till the municipal corporation was ended, as the City of Adelaide was too poor to maintain the machinery; but 75 pounds was the rent of the house and yards. We sold the cows, and my brothers went farming, and we took cheaper quarters in Halifax street.

The Town Clerkship, however, was the means of giving me a lesson in electoral methods. Into the Municipal Bill, drawn up under the superintendence of Rowland Hill (afterward the great post office reformer, but then the Secretary of the Colonization Commissioner for South Australia), he had introduced a clause providing for proportional representation at the option of the ratepayers. The twentieth part of the Adelaide ratepayers by uniting their votes upon one man instead of voting for 18, could on the day before the ordinary election appear and declare this their intention, and he would be a Councillor on their votes. In the first election, November, 1840, two such quorums elected two Councillors. The workmen in Borrow and Goodear's building elected their foreman, and another quorum of citizens elected Mr. William Senden; and this was the first quota representation in the world. My father explained this unique provision to me at the time, and showed its bearings for minority representation.

After the break up of the municipality and the loss of his income my father lost health and spirits. The brothers did not succeed in the country. My sister had married Andrew Murray, an apparently prosperous man, in 1841, but the protecting of the Government bills bought for remitting to England, and other causes, brought down every mercantile firm in Adelaide except A. L. Elder, who had not been long established; and Murray & Greig came down too. Mr. Murray was a ready writer, and got work on The South Australian, the newspaper which supported Capt. Grey's policy of retrenchment and stoppage of public works; so, with a small salary, he managed to live. When I left Scotland I brought with me a letter of recommendation from my teacher, Miss Sarah Phin, concerning my qualifications and my turn for teaching. I don't know if it really did me any good, for the suspicious look and the question about how old I was at the time embarrassed me. Of course I was only 13 1/2 and probably my teacher over-estimated me a little, but here is, the letter, yellow with the dust of over 70 years.

Melrose. June 20, 1839.

My dearest Catherine—Our mutual friend, Mrs. Duncan, told me that you were not to sail for Australia till next month, and I have been thinking if my poor testimonial to your worth and abilities could be of any service to you I ought to give it but how can I trust myself?—for could any one read what I feel my heart dictates it would be thought absurd. You were always one of the greatest ornaments of my school, best girl and the best scholar, and from the time you could put three letters together you have evinced a turn for teaching—so clear-headed and so patient, and so thoroughly upright in word and deed, and your knowledge of the Scriptures equal to that of many students of Divinity, so should you ever become a teacher you have nothing to fear. You will be able to undertake both the useful and the ornamental branches of education—French, Italian, and Music you thoroughly understand. I feel conscious that you will succeed. Please to remember me to your excellent mother, and with love to Miss

Spence and my darling Mary, believe me, my beloved Catherine, your affectionate friend and teacher. Sarah Phin.

My knowledge of music was not great, even in those days, but I could teach beginners for two or three years with fair success. We thought that my mother and the two eldest girls could start a school, and brought out with us a good selection of schoolbooks, bought from Oliver J. Boyd. Edinburgh, superior to the English books obtainable here, which we used up in time; but we dared not launch out into such a venture in 1840, and my sister Jessie had no desire to teach at all. The years at Brownhill Creek and West terrace were the most unhappy of my life. I suffered from the want of some intellectual activity, and from the sense of frustrated ambition and religious despair. The few books we had, or which we could borrow, I read over and over again. Aikin's "British Poets," a gift from Uncle John Spence, and Goldsmith's complete works, a school prize of my brother William's, were thoroughly mastered, and the Waverley novels down to "Quentin Durward" were well absorbed. I read in Chambers's Journal of daily governesses getting a shilling an hour, and I told my friend, Mrs. Haining, that I would go out for 6d. an hour. Although she disliked that way of putting it, it was really on that basis that I had made my beginning when I reached the age of 17. In the meantime I had taught my younger sister Mary (afterwards Mrs. W. J. Wren) all I knew, and in the columns of The South Australian I wrote an occasional letter or a few verses. Through Mr. George Tinline we made the acquaintance of Mrs. Samuel Stephens her brother, Thomas Hudson Beare, and his family, who had all come out in the Duke of York, and lived six months on Kangaroo Island before South Australia was proclaimed a British province. I have been mixed up so much with this family that it is often supposed that they were relatives, but it was not so. Samuel Stephens had died from an accident two years after his marriage to a lady much older and much richer than himself, and she was living on two acres in North Adelaide, bought with her money at the first sale of city lands in 1837, and Mr. Tinline boarded with her till his marriage. The nephews, and especially the nieces, of the old lady interested me—Lucy, the eldest, a handsome girl, was about two years younger than myself; Arabella, about the age of my sister

Mary; Elizabeth, the baby Beare, who was the first white person to set foot on South Australian soil after the foundation of the province, died from a burning accident when quite young. The only survivor of that first family now is William L. Beare (84), held in honour as one of our earliest pioneers. By a second marriage there were nine more children. Several died young, but some still survive.

It was not till 1843 that I went as a daily governess at the rate of 6d. an hour, and gave two hours five days a week to the families of the Postmaster-General, the Surveyor-General, and the Private Secretary. Thus I earned three guineas a month. I don't recollect taking holidays, except a week at Christmas. I enjoyed the work, and I was proud of the payment. My mother said she never felt the bitterness of poverty after I began to earn money, and the shyness which, in spite of all her instructions and encouragement, I had felt with all strangers, disappeared when I felt independent. When a girl is very poor, and feels herself badly dressed, she cannot help being shy, especially if she has a good deal of Scotch pride. I think mother felt more sorry for me in those early days than for the others, because I was so ambitious, and took religious difficulties so hard. How old I felt at 17. Indeed, at 14 I felt quite grown up. In 1843 I felt I had begun the career in Australia that I had anticipated in Scotland. I was trusted to teach little girls, and they interested me, each individual with a difference. I had seen things I had written in print. If I was one of the oldest in feeling of the young folk in South Australia in my teens, I am the youngest woman in feeling in my eighties; so I have had abundant compensation.

CHAPTER IV
LOVERS AND FRIENDS

It is always supposed that thoughts of love and marriage are the chief concerns in a girl's life, but it was not the case with me. I had only two offers of marriage in my life, and I refused both. The first might have been accepted if it had not been for the Calvinistic creed that made me shrink from the possibility of bringing children into the world with so little chance of eternal salvation, so I said. "No" to a very clever young man, with whom I had argued on many points, and with whom, if I had married him, I should have argued till one of us died! I was 17, and had just begun to earn money. I told him why I had refused him, and that it was final. In six weeks he was engaged to another woman. My second offer was made to me when I was 23 by a man aged 55, with three children. He was an artist, whose second wife and several children had been murdered by the Maoris near Wanganui during the Maori insurrection of the forties, and he had come to Adelaide with the three survivors. The massacre of that family was only one of the terrible tragedies of that time, but it was not the less shocking. The Maoris had never been known to kill a woman, and when the house was attacked, Mr. Gilfillan got out of a back window to call the soldiers to their help. Though struck on the back of the head and the neck and scarred for life—owing to which he was always compelled to wear his hair long—he succeeded in his mission. His wife put her own two children through the window, and they toddled off hand in hand until they met their father returning with the soldiers. The eldest daughter, a girl of 13, escaped with a neighbour's child, a baby in arms. She was seen by the Maoris, struck on the forehead with a stone axe, and left unconscious. The crying of the baby roused her, and she went to the cowyard and milked a cow to get milk for the hungry child, and there she was found by the soldiers. She was queer in her ways and thoughts afterwards, and, it was said, always remained 13 years old. She died in November last, aged 74. Her stepmother and the baby and her own brother and sister were murdered one by one as they tried to escape by the same window that had led the rest of the family to safety. One of the toddling survivors still lives in New Zealand. Now, these are all the chances of marriage I have had in my life. Dickens, in "David Copperfield," speaks of an old maid who keeps the remembrance of some one who might have made her an offer, the shadowy Pidger, in her heart until her death. I cannot forget these two men. I am constantly meeting with the children, grandchildren, and even great-grandchildren of the first. As for the other, Andrew Murray gave me a fine landscape painted by John A. Gilfillan as a slight acknowledgment of services rendered to his newspaper when he left it to go to Melbourne, and it hangs up in my sitting room for all to see. Mr. Gilfillan had a commission to paint "The Landing of Capt. Cook" with the help of Portraits and miniatures of the principal personages, and some sketches of his of Adelaide in 1849 are in the Adelaide Art Gallery. If the number of lovers has been few, no woman in Australia has been richer in friends. This narrative will show what good friends—men as well as women—have helped me and sympathized in my work and my aims. I believe that if I had been in love, especially if I had been disappointed in love, my novels would have been stronger and more interesting; but I kept a watch over myself, which I felt I knew I needed, for I was both imaginative and affectionate. I did not want to give my heart away. I did not desire a love disappointment, even for the sake of experience. I was 30 years old before the dark veil of religious despondency was completely lifted from my soul, and by that time I felt myself booked for a single life. People married young if they married at all in those days. The single aunts put on caps at 30 as a sort of signal that they accepted their fate; and, although I did not do so, I felt a good deal the same.

I went on with daily teaching for some years, during which my father's health declined, but before his death two things had happened to cheer him. My brother John left Myponga and came to town, and obtained a clerkship in the South Australian Bank at 100 pounds a year. It was whilst occupying a position in the bank that he had some slight connection with the notorious Capt. Starlight, afterwards the hero of "Robbery Under Arms," for through his hands much of the stolen money passed. In 1900, when Mrs. Young and I were leaving Melbourne on our visit to Sydney, we were introduced to "Rolf Boldrewood," the author of that well-known story. His grave face lit up with a smile when my friend referred to the author of her son's hero. "Ah!" and he shook his head slowly. "I'm not quite sure about the wisdom of making heroes of such sorry stuff," he replied. I thought I could do better with a school. I was 20, and my sister Mary nearly 16, and my mother could help. My school opened in May, 1846, a month before my father's death, and he thought that our difficulties were over. My younger brother, David Wauchope, had been left behind for his education with the three maiden aunts, but he came out about the end of that year, and began life in the office of the Burra Mine at a small salary. My eldest brother William, was not successful in the country, and went to Western Australia for some years, and later to New Zealand, where he died in his eightieth year, soon after the death of my brother John in his seventy-ninth, leaving me the only survivor of eight born and of six who grew to full age. My eldest sister Agnes died of consumption at the age of 16; and, as my father's mother and four of his brothers and sisters had died of this malady, it was supposed to be in the family. The only time I was kept out of school during the nine years at Miss Phin's was when I was 12 when I had a cough and suppuration of the glands of the neck. As this was the way in which Agnes's illness had begun, my parents were alarmed, though I had no idea of it. I was leeched and blistered and drugged; I was put into flannel for the only time in my life; I was sent away for change of air; but no one could discover that the cough was from the lungs. It passed away with the cold weather, and I cannot say that I have had any illness since. My father died of decline, but, if he had been more fortunate, I think he would have lived much longer. Probably my mother's life was prolonged beyond that of a long-lived family by her coming to Australia in middle life; and if I ever had any tendency to consumption, the climate must have helped me. There were no special precautions against infection in those days: but no other member of the family took it, and the alarm about me was three years after Agnes's death.

But to go on to those early days of the forties. There were two families with whom we were intimate. Mr. George Tinline (who had been clerk to my fathers' old friend, William Rutherford, of Jedburgh), who was in the bank of South Australia when in 1839, my father went to put our small funds in safety, introduced us to a beautiful young widow, Mrs. Sharpe, and her sisters Eliza and Harriet, and her brother, John Taylor. Harriet afterwards married Edward Stirling, a close friend of my brother-in-law, Andrew Murray, and I was a great deal interested in the Stirlings and their eight children. Mr. William Bakewell, of Bartley & Bakewell, solicitors, married Jane Warren of Springfield, Barossa, and I was a familiar friend of their five children. In one house I was "Miss Spence, the storyteller," in the other "Miss Spence, the teller of tales!" Some of the tales appeared long after as Christmas stories in The Adelaide Observer, but my young hearers preferred the oral narrative, with appropriate gestures and emphasis, and had no scruple about making faces, to anything printed in books. I took great liberties with what I had read and sometimes invented all. It was a part of their education, probably—certainly, it was a part of mine, and it gave me a command of language which helped me when I became a public speaker. My brother-in-law's newspaper furnished an occasional opportunity to me, though no doubt he considered that he could fill his twice-a-week journal without my help. He was, however, helpful in other ways. He was one of the subscribers to a Reading Club, and through him I had access to newspapers and magazines. The South Australian Institute was a treasure to the family. I recollect a newcomer being astonished at my sister Mary having read Macaulay's History. "Why, it was only just out when I left England," said he. "Well, it did not take longer to come out than you did," was her reply. We were all omnivorous readers, and the old-fashioned accomplishment of reading aloud was cultivated by both brothers and sisters. I was the only one who could translate French at sight, thanks to Miss Phin's giving me so much of Racine and Moliere and other good French authors in my school days.

But more important than all this was the fact that we took hold of the growth and development of South Australia, and identified ourselves with it. Nothing is insignificant in the history of a young community, and—above all—nothing seems impossible. I had learned what wealth was, and a great deal about production and exchange for myself in the early history of South Australia—of the value of machinery, of roads and bridges, and of ports for transport and export. I had seen the 4-lb. loaf at 4/ and at 4d. I had seen Adelaide the dearest and the cheapest place to live in. I had seen money orders for 2/6, and even for 6d., current when gold and silver were very scarce. Even before the discovery of copper South Australia had turned the corner. We had gone on the land and become primary producers, and before the gold discoveries in Victoria revolutionized Australia and attracted our male population across the border, the Central State was the only one which had a large surplus of wheat and hay to send to the goldfields.

Edward Wilson of The Argus, riding overland to Adelaide about 1848, was amazed to see from Willunga onward fenced and cultivated farms, with decent homesteads and machinery up to date. The Ridley stripper enabled our people to reap and thresh the corn when hands were all too few for the sickle. He said he felt as if the garden of Paradise must have been in King William street and that the earliest difference in the world—that between Cain and Abel—was about the advantages of the 80-acre system. Australia generally had already to realize the fact that the pastoral industry was not enough for its development, and South Australia had seemed to solve the problem through the doctrinaire founders, of family immigration, small estates, and the development of agriculture, horticulture, and viticulture. We owed a great deal in the latter branches to our German settlers—sent out originally by Mr. G. F. Angas, whose interest was aroused by their suffering persecution for religious dissent—who saw that Australia had a better climate than that of the Fatherland. We owed much to Mr. George Stevenson, who was an enthusiastic gardener and fruitgrower, and lectured on these subjects, but the contrast between the environs of Adelaide and those of Sydney and Melbourne were striking, and Mr. Wilson never lost an opportunity of calling on the Victorian Legislature and the Victorian public to develop their own wonderful resources. When you take gold out of the ground there is less gold to win. When you grow golden grain or ruddy grapes this year you may expect as much and as good next year. My brother David went with the thousands to buy their fortunes at the diggings, but my brother John stuck to the Bank of South Australia. My brother-in-law's subscribers and his printers had gone off and left him woefully embarrassed. He went to Melbourne. My friend John Taylor left his sheep in the wilderness and came to Adelaide to the aid of The Register. He had been engaged to Sophia Stephens, who died, and her father John Stephens also died soon after; and Mr. Taylor shouldered the management of the paper until the time of stress was over.

When Andrew Murray obtained employment on The Argus as commercial editor, he left his twice-a-week newspaper in the charge of Mr. W. W. Whitridge, my brother John, and myself. If anything was needed to be written on State aid to religion I was to do it, as Mr. Whitridge was opposed to it. This lasted three months. The next quarter there were no funds for the editor, so John and I carried it on, and then let it die. At that time I believed in State aid, which had been abolished by the first elected Parliament of South Australia, although that Parliament consisted of one-third nominees pledged to vote for its continuance.

CHAPTER V
NOVELS AND A POLITICAL INSPIRATION

It was the experience of a depopulated province which led me to write my first book, "Clara Morison—A Tale of South Australia during the Gold Fever." I entrusted the M.S. to my friend John Taylor, with whom I had just had the only tiff in my life. He, through his connection with The Register, knew that I was writing in The South Australian, trying to keep it alive, till Mr. Murray decided to let it go, and he told this to other people. At a subscription ball to which my brother John took me and my younger sister Mary, she found she had been pointed out and talked of as the lady who wrote for the newspapers. I did not like it even to be supposed of myself, but Mary was indignant, and I wrote an injured letter to my friend. He apologized, and said he thought I would be proud of doing disinterested work, and he was sorry the mistake had been made regarding the sister who did it. Of course, I forgave him. He was the last man in the world to give pain to anyone, and I highly admired him for his disinterested work on The Register. He reluctantly accepted 1,000 pounds when the paper was sold. He must have lost much more through neglect of his own affairs at such a critical time. He was taking a holiday with his sister Eliza in England and France, where the beautiful widowed sister was settled as Madam Dubois, and I asked him to take "Clara Morison" to Smith, Elder & Co.'s, in London, and to say nothing to anybody about it; but before it was placed he had to return to Adelaide, and in pursuance of my wishes, left it with my other good friend, Mr. Bakewell, who also happened to be visiting England with his family at the time—1853-4. I had an idea that, as there was so much interest in Australia and its gold, I might get 100 pounds for the novel. Mr. Bakewell wrote a preface from which I extract a passage:—"The writer's aim seems to have been to present some picture of the state of society in South Australia in the years 1851-2, when the discovery of gold in the neighbouring province of Victoria took place. At this time, the population of South Australia numbered between seventy and eighty thousand souls, the greater part of whom were remarkable for their intelligence, their industry, and their enterprise, which, in the instance of the Burra Burra, and other copper mines had met with such signal success. When it became known that gold in vast quantities could be found within 300 miles of their own territory, they could not remain unmoved. The exodus was almost complete, and entirely without parallel. In those days there was no King in Israel, and every woman did what was right in her own sight." Another reason I had for writing the book. Thackeray had written about an emigrant vessel taking a lot of women to Australia, as if these were all to be gentlemen's wives—as if there was such a scarcity of educated women there, that anything wearing petticoats had the prospect of a great rise in position. I had hoped that Smith, Elder, & Co. would publish my book, but their reader—Mr. Williams, who discovered Charlotte Bronte's genius when she sent them "The Professor," and told her she could write a better, which she did ("Jane Eyre")—wrote a similar letter to me, declining "Clara Morison," as he had declined "The Professor," but saying I could do better. J. W. Parker & Son published it in 1854, as one of the two-volume series, of which "The Heir of Redcliffe" had been most successful. The price was to be 40 pounds; but, as it was too long for the series, I was charged 10 pounds for abridging it. It was very fairly received and reviewed. I think I liked best Frederick Sinnett's notice in The Argus—that it was the work of an observant woman—a novelist who happened to live in Australia, but who did not labour to bring in bushrangers and convicts, and specially Australian features. While I was waiting to hear the fate of my first book, I began to write a second, "Tender and True," of which Mr. Williams thought better, and recommended it to Smith, Elder, and Co., who published it in two volumes in 1856, and gave me 20 pounds for the copyright. This is the only one of my books that went through more than one edition. There were two or three large editions issued, but I never got a penny more. I was told that nothing could be made out of shilling editions; but that book was well reviewed and now and then I have met elderly people who read the cheap edition and liked it. The motif of the book was the jealousy which husbands are apt to feel of their wives' relations. As if the most desirable wife was an amiable orphan—if an heiress, so much the better. But the domestic virtues which make a happy home for the husband are best fostered in a centre where brothers and sisters have to give and take; and a good daughter and sister is likely to make a good wife and mother. I have read quite recently that the jokes against the mother-in-law which are so many and so bitter in English and American journalism are worn out, and have practically ceased; but Dickens and Thackeray set the fashion, and it lasted a long time.

While "Clara Morison" was making her debut, I paid my first visit to Melbourne. I went with Mr. and Mrs. Stirling in a French ship consigned to him, and we were 12 days on the way, suffering from the limited ideas that the captain of a French merchantman had of the appetites of Australians at sea. I intended to pay a six weeks' visit to my sister and her family, but she was so unwell that I stayed for eight months. I found that Melbourne in the beginning of 1854 was a very expensive place to live in, and consequently a very inhospitable place. Mr. Murray's salary sounded a good one, 500 pounds a year, but it did not get much comfort. His sister was housekeeper at Charles Williamson & Co.'s, and that was the only place where I could take off my bonnet and have a meal. From the windows I watched the procession that welcomed Sir Charles Hotham, the first Governor of the separated colony of Victoria. He was received with rejoicing, but he utterly failed to satisfy the people. He thought anything was good enough for them. One festivity I was invited to—a ball given on the opening of the new offices of The Argus in Collins street—and there I met Mr. Edward Wilson, a most interesting personality, the giver of the entertainment. He was then vigorously championing the unlocking of the land and the developing of other resources of Victoria than the gold. It had surprised him when he travelled overland to Adelaide to see from Willunga 30 miles of enclosed and cultivated farms, and it surprised me to see sheepruns close to Melbourne. With a better rainfall and equally good soil, Victoria had neither the farms nor the vineyards nor the orchards nor the gardens that had sprung up under the 80-acre section and immigration systems of South Australia. It had been an outlying portion of New South Wales, neglected and exploited for pastoral settlement only. The city, however, had been well planned, like that of Adelaide, but the suburbs were allowed to grow anyhow. In Adelaide the belt of park lands kept the city apart from all suburbs. Andrew Murray was as keen for the development of Victoria agriculturally and industrially as Mr. Wilson, and they worked together heartily. Owing to the state of my sister's health I was much occupied with her and her children; but in August she was well, and I returned with Mr. Taylor and his sister in the steamer Bosphorus, when it touched at Melbourne on the way home. He brought me 30 pounds for my book, and the assurance that it would be out soon, and that I should have six copies to give to my friends. Novel writing had not been to me a lucrative occupation. I had given up teaching altogether at the age of 25, and I felt that, though Australia was to be a great country, there was no market for literary work, and the handicap of distance from the reading world was great.

My younger sister married in 1855 William J. Wren, then an articled clerk in Bartley & Bakewell's office, and afterwards a partner with the present Sir James Boucaut. Mr. Wren's health was indifferent, and caused us much anxiety. My brother John married Jessie Cumming in 1858, and they were spared together for many years. As the Wrens went on a long voyage to Hongkong and back for the sake of my brother-in-law's health, my mother and I had the charge of their little boy. But in that year, 1859, my mind received its strongest political inspiration, and the reform of the electoral system became the foremost object of my life. John Stuart Mill's advocacy of Thomas Hare's system of proportional representation brought back to my mind Rowland Hill's clause in the Adelaide Municipal Bill with wider and larger issues. It also showed me how democratic government could be made real, and safe, and progressive. I confess that at first I was struck chiefly by its conservative side, and I saw that its application would prevent the political association, which corresponded roughly with the modern Labour Party, from returning five out of six members of the Assembly for the City of Adelaide. But for blunders on ballot papers the whole ticket of six would have been elected. They also elected the three members for Burra, and Clare. I had then no footing on the Adelaide press, but I was Adelaide correspondent for The Melbourne Argus—that is to say, my brother was the correspondent, but I wrote the letters—he furnished the news. I read Mill's article one Monday night, and wrote what was meant for a leader on Tuesday morning, and went to read it to my brother at breakfast time, and posted it forthwith. I knew The Argus had been dissatisfied with the recent elections, and fancied that the editor would hail with joy the new idea; but I received the reply that The Argus was committed to the representation of majorities; and, though the idea was ingenious, he did not even offer to print it as a letter. About two years later Mr. Lavington Glyde, M.P., brought forward in the Assembly Mr. Fawcett's abstract of Hare's great scheme, and I seized the opportunity of writing a series of letters to The Register, signed by my initials. Mr. Glyde, seeing the House did not like his suggestions, dropped the matter, but I did not. I was no longer correspondent to The Argus—the telegraph stopped that altogether. My wonderful maiden aunts made up to me and my mother the 50 pounds a year that I had received as correspondent, and did as much for their brother, Alexander Brodie, of Morphett Vale, from 1,000 pounds they had sent to invest in South Australia. It was as easy to get 10 per cent. then as to get 4 per cent. now; indeed I think the money earned 12 per cent. at first. My brother John was accountant to the South Australian Railways, then not a very great department—I think the line stretched as far as Kapunda to the north from Port Adelaide. He was as much captivated by Mr. Hare's idea as I was, and he said that if I would write a pamphlet he would pay for the printing of 1,000 copies, to be sent to all the members of Parliament and other leading people in city and country. I called my pamphlet "A Plea for Pure Democracy," and when writing it I felt the democratic strength of the position as I had not felt it in reading Hare's own book. It cost my brother 15 pounds, but he never grudged it.

While the pamphlet was in the press, I heard of the dangerous illness of my friend Lucy Anne Duval (nee Beare), one of the original passengers in the Duke of York, the first ship which arrived here. I went to consult Mr. Taylor and Mr. Stirling at their office. I saw only Mr. Stirling. I said, "I should like to go and nurse her," and he said. "If you will go, I'll pay your expenses;" and I went and stayed with her for three weeks, till she died, and left five children, three of them quite young. There were Duvals in England in good circumstances, and I wrote pleading for the three little ones, though every one said it was quite useless; but an uncle by marriage was touched, and sent 100 pounds a year for the benefit of the three children, and I was constituted the guardian. The youngest died within two years, but the allowance was not decreased, and I was able to get some schooling for an elder boy. This was my first guardianship.

My pamphlet did not set the Torrens on fire. It did not convert The Register, but Mr. Fred Sinnett, who was conducting The Telegraph, was much impressed, especially as he had the greatest reverence for John Stuart Mill, and thought him a safe man to follow. I had another novel under way at the time, and Mr. Sinnett thought it would help The Telegraph to bring it out as a serial story in the weekly edition; and I seized my opportunity to bring in Mr. Hare and proportional representation. In England Mr. Hare, Mr. Mill, Rowland Hill, and his brother, and Professor Craik, all considered my "Plea for Pure Democracy" the best argument from the popular side that had appeared. I got the kindest of letters from them, and my brother considered my labour and his money well spent. Professor Craik, writing to Miss Florence Davenport Hill about the "Plea for Pure Democracy," says—"It is really a pity that the pamphlet should not be reproduced in this country—modified, of course, to the slight extent that would be necessary. It is really a very remarkable piece of exposition—the best for popular effect by far on this subject that has come in my way. I rejoice to hear that there is a chance of Mr. Hare's plan being adopted in South Australia." I may be allowed to observe that there is still a chance, but not yet a reality. My aunts at Thornton Loch were applied to by my English admirers to see if they would be at the cost of an English edition; but, though they were goodness itself to our material needs, they thought it was throwing money away to bring out a pamphlet on an unpopular subject that would not sell. Why, even in South Australia, though the price was marked at one shilling, not a single shilling had been paid for a single copy; and in South

Australia I was known! Not so well known, however. I wrote under initials only, and many thought my letters and pamphlets were the work of Charles Simeon Hare, one of the tallest talkers in South Australia, who said Mr. Thomas Hare was his cousin. My novels were anonymous up to the third, which was not then written. If my name would have done the cause any good it would have been given, but it was too obscure then.

    The original title of my third book was "Uphill Work," and it took up the woman question as it appeared to me at the time—the difficulty of a woman earning a livelihood, even when she had as much ability, industry, and perseverance as a man. My friend Mrs. Graham, who had been receiving 100 pounds a year and many presents and much consideration from the Alstons, of Charles Williamson & Co., had to return to Scotland to cheer her father's last years. After his death she became housekeeper to the Crichton Asylum for the Insane, with 600 or 700 patients, at a salary of 30 pounds a year. This started me on the story of two girls educated well and soundly by an eccentric uncle, but not accomplished in the showy branches, who, fearing that the elder and favourite niece would marry a young neighbour, and that the other might be a confirmed invalid, disinherited them, and left his estate to a natural son with a strict proviso against his marrying either of his cousins. In that case the property was to go to a benevolent institution named. Jane Melville applied for the situation of housekeeper to this institution at 30 pounds a year, but was refused because she was too young and inexperienced. After all sorts of disappointments she took a situation to go out to Australia, and her sister accompanied her as a lady's maid in the same family. You may wonder how I brought in proportional representation, but I managed it. I think, on the whole, it is a stronger book than either of the others. The volume has two interesting associations, one which connects it with Mrs. Oliphant. My friend Mrs. Graham knew I had sent it to England for publication, and when she read the anonymous "Doctor's Family" she was sure it was mine, and was delighted with it. When I read of the brave Australian girl Nettie, taking on herself the burden of the flabby sister and her worthless husband and their children, I wished that I had written such a capital story. In a subsequent tale of Mrs. Oliphant's, "In Trust," a father disinherits the elder girl from a fear of an unworthy marriage, but he leaves a letter to be opened when Rosy is 21, which—should Anne not marry Cosmo Douglas—restores her to her own mother's fortune, which was in his power. There was no saving clause in my book. The nieces were left only 20 pounds a year each. Mr. Williams did not think "Uphill Work" as good as "Tender and True," and it was hung up till circumstances most unexpectedly brought me to England, and I tried Bentley, and found that his reader approved, but wished me to change the name, as the first critic would say it was uphill work to read it. Then let it be "Mr. Haliburton's Will." That would clash with "Mrs Haliburton's Troubles." So the name was changed to Hogarth, and the title became "Mr. Hogarth's Will." It was well reviewed, and I got 35 pounds as my half-share of the profits on a three-volume edition, besides 50 pounds from The Telegraph. But the book was to have more effect in unexpected quarters than I could imagine. When staying with my aunts in Scotland I had a letter from Mr. Edward Wilson's secretary, saying that he had wished to write an article for The Fortnightly on "The Representation of Classes," which was his cure for the excesses of democracy; but, as he could not see, and his doctor had forbidden him even to dictate, he had reluctantly abandoned the idea. He had, however, heard that I was in Scotland, and, though my idea was different from his, he believed that I could write the article from some letters reprinted from The Argus and a few hints from himself, and that I could adapt them to English conditions. I gladly undertook the work, and satisfied Mr. Wilson. Just before I left for Australia I went to Mr. Wilson's, and we went through the proofs together. Mr. Wilson, being a wealthy man, did not ask any payment from The Fortnightly, but he gave me 10 pounds and thanked me for stepping in to his assistance when he needed it. He said that my novel had been the subject of a great deal of discussion in his house. I asked, "Why?" He replied, "The uncle and the nieces, of course." I thought no more of it till the death of Mr. Wilson revealed that he had left his estate to the charities of Melbourne. Then my brother told me that when he was in England in 1877 Mr. Wilson had told him that it was seldom that a novel had any influence over a man's conduct, but that reading his sister's novel had set him thinking, and had made him alter his will. He did not think it to the advantage of his nieces to be made rich, and he would leave his money to Victoria and Melbourne, where he had made it. I was the innocent cause of disappointing the nieces, for I think I made it clear that the uncle did very wrongly. But when I see 5,000 pounds a year distributed among Melbourne charities, and larger gifts for the building of a new hospital, I cannot help thinking that these are the results of Mr. Wilson reading "Mr. Hogarth's Will" and it may be that other similar trusts are the results of Mr. Wilson's action.

Another literary success I had during that visit to England. I went to Smith, Elder, & Co. to ask if I could not get anything for the shilling edition of "Tender and True," and was answered in the negative; but I had not talked ten minutes with Mr. Williams before he said that if I would put these ideas into shape, he thought he could get an article accepted by The Cornhill Magazine. "An Australian's Impressions of England" was approved by the editor, and appeared in The Cornhill for January 1866, and for that I received 12 pounds, the best-paid work I had ever had up to that time. The Saturday Review said of "Mr. Hogarth's Will" that there was no haziness about money matters in it such as is too common among lady writers. Mr. Bentley advised me to give my name, and not to sell my copyright; but the latter has been of no value to me; 500 copies of a three-volume novel exhausted the likely demand. I got 12 copies to give to friends, and one copy I gave to Mr. Hare. His daughters were a little amused to see their father in a novel, and as the book was in the circulating library their friends and acquaintances used to ask, "Is that really your papa that it is intended for?" I did not at the time think of facing anybody in England, but I had been both amused and annoyed with the portraits I was supposed to have drawn from real people in and about Adelaide—often people I had never seen and had not beard of. "But Harris is Ellis to the life," said my old Aunt Brodie of Morphett Vale. "Miss Withing is my sister-in-law," said another. Neither of these people had I seen. Of course, Mr. Reginald was Mr. John Taylor, the only squatter I knew, but I myself was not identified with my heroine Clara Morison. I was Margaret Elliott, the girl who was studying law with her brother

Gilbert; but my brother and my cousin Louisa Brodie were supposed to be figuring in my book as lovers. In a small society it was easy to affix the characteristics to some one whom it was possible the author might have met; but I shrank from the idea that I was capable of "taking off" people of my acquaintance, and for many reasons would have liked if the book had not been known to be mine in South Australia. There must, however, have been some lifelike presentment of my characters, or they could not have been recognised. About this time I read and appreciated Jane Austen's novels—those exquisite miniatures, which no doubt her contemporaries identified without much interest. Her circle was as narrow as mine—indeed, narrower. She was the daughter of a clergyman in the country. She represented well-to-do grownup people, and them alone. The humour of servants, the sallies of children, the machinations of villains, the tricks of rascals, are not on her canvas; but she differentiated among equals with a firm hand, and with a constant ripple of amusement. The life I led had more breadth and wider interests. The life of Miss Austen's heroines, though delightful to read about, would have been deadly dull to endure. So great a charm have Jane Austen's books had for me that I have made a practice of reading them through regularly once a year.

As we grew to love South Australia, we felt that we were in an expanding society, still feeling the bond to the motherland, but eager to develop a perfect society, in the land of our adoption.

CHAPTER VI
A TRIP TO ENGLAND

I have gone on with the story of my three first novels consecutively, anticipating the current history of myself and South Australia. There were three great steps taken in the development of Australia. The first was when McArthur introduced the merino sheep; the second when Hargreaves and others discovered gold; and the latest when cold-storage was introduced to make perishable products available for the European markets. The second step created a sudden revolution; but the others were gradual, and the area of alluvial diggings in Victoria made thousands of men without capital or machinery rush to try their fortunes—first from the adjacent colonies, and afterwards from the ends of the earth. Law and order were kept on the goldfields of Mount Alexander, Bendigo, and Ballarat by means of a strong body of police, and the high licence fees for claims paid for their services, so that nothing like the scenes recorded of the Californian diggings could be permitted. But for the time ordinary industries were paralysed. Shepherds left their flocks, farmers their land, clerks their desks, and artisans their trades. Melbourne grew apace in spite of the highest wages known being exacted by masons and carpenters. Pastoralists thought ruin stared them in the face till they found what a market the goldfields offered for their surplus stock. Our South Australian farmers left their holdings in the hands of their wives and children too young to take with them, but almost all of them returned to grow grain and produce to send to Victoria. It was astonishing what the women had done during their absence. The fences were kept repaired and the stock attended to, the grapes gathered, and the wine made. In these days it was not so easy to get 80 acres or more in Victoria; so, with what the farmers brought from their labours on the goldfields, they extended their holdings and improved their homes. For many years the prices in Melbourne regulated prices in Adelaide, but when the land was unlocked and the Victorian soil and climate were found to be as good as ours it was Mark lane that fixed prices over all Australia for primary products. After the return of most of the diggers there was a great deal of marrying and giving in marriage. The miners who had left the Burra for goldseeking gradually came back, and the nine remarkable copper mines of Moonta and Wallaroo attracted the Cornishmen, who preferred steady wages and homes to the diminishing chances of Ballarat and Bendigo where machinery and deep sinking demanded capital, and the miners were paid by the week. These new copper mines were found in the Crown leases held by Capt. (afterwards Sir Walter) Hughes. He had been well dealt with by Elder, Smith, & Co., and gave them the opportunity of supporting him. At that time my friends Edward Stirling and John Taylor were partners in that firm, and they shared in the success. Mr. Bakewell belonged to the legal firm which did their business, so that my greatest friends seemed to be in it. I think my brother John profited less by the great advance of South Australia than he deserved for sticking to the Bank of South Australia. He got small rises in his salary, but the cost of living was so enhanced that at the end of seven years it did not buy much more than the 100 pounds he had begun with. My eldest maiden aunt died, and left to her brother and sister in South Australia all she had in her power. My mother bought a brick cottage in Pulteney street and a Burra share with her legacy—both excellent investments—and my brother left the bank and went into the aerated water business with James Hamilton Parr.

We made the acquaintance of the family of Mrs. Francis Clark, of Hazelwood, Burnside. She was the only sister of five clever brothers—Matthew Davenport, Rowland, Edwin, Arthur, and Frederick Hill. Rowland is best known, but all were remarkable men. She was so like my mother in her sound judgment, accurate observation, and kind heart, that I was drawn to her at once. But it was Miss Clark who sought an introduction to me at a ball, because her uncle Rowland had written to her that "Clara Morison," the new novel, was a capital story of South Australian life. She was the first person to seek me out on account of literary work, and I was grateful to her. I think all the brothers Hill wrote books, and Rosamond and Florence Davenport Hill had just published "Our Exemplars." My friendship with Miss Clark led to much work together, and the introduction was a great widening of interests for me. There were four sons and three daughters—Miss Clark and Howard were the most literary, but all had great ability and intelligence. They were Unitarians, and W. J. Wren, my brother-in-law, was also a Unitarian, and had been one of the 12 Adelaide citizens who invited out a minister and guaranteed his salary. I was led to hear what the Rev. J. Crawford Woods had to say for that faith, and told my old minister (Rev. Robert Haining) that for three months I would hear him in the morning and Mr. Woods in the evening, and read nothing but the Bible as my guide; and by that time I would decide. I had been induced to go to the Sacrament at 17, with much heart searching, but when I was 25 I said I could not continue a communicant, as I was not a converted Christian. This step greatly surprised both Mr. and Mrs. Haining, as I did not propose to leave the church. The result of my three months' enquiry was that I became a convinced Unitarian, and the cloud was lifted from the universe. I think I have been a most cheerful person ever since. My mother was not in any way distressed, though she never separated from the church of her fathers. My brother was as completely converted as I was, and he was happy in finding a wife like minded. My sister, Mrs. Wren, also was satisfied with the new faith; so that she and her husband saw eye to eye. It was a very live congregation in those early days. We liked our pastor, and we admired his wife, and there were a number of interesting and clever people who went to the Wakefield Street Church.

It was rather remarkable that my sister's husband and my brother's wife arrived on the same day in two different ships—one in the Anglier from England, and the other in the Three Bells from Glasgow—in 1851; but I did not make the acquaintance of either till 1854 and 1855. Jessie Cumming and Mary Spence shook hands and formed a friendship over Carlyle's "Sartor Resartus." My brother-in-law (W. J. Wren) had fine literary tastes, especially for poetry. The first gift to his wife after marriage was Elizabeth Browning's poems in two volumes and Robert Browning's "Plays and Dramatic Lyrics" in two volumes, and Mary and I delighted in them all. In those days I considered my sister Mary and my sister-in-law the most brilliant conversationalists I knew. My elder sister, Mrs. Murray, also talked very well—so much so that her husband's friends and visitors fancied she must write a lot of his articles; but none of the three ladies went beyond writing good letters. I think all of them were keener of sight than I was—more observant of features, dress, and manners; but I took in more by the ear. As Sir Walter Scott says, "Speak that I may know thee." To my mind, dialogue is more important for a novel than description; and, if you have a firm grasp of your characters, the dialogue will be true. With me the main difficulty was the plot; and I was careful that this should not be merely possible, but probable. I have heard scores of people say that they have got good plots in their heads, and when pressed to tell them they proved to be only incidents. You need much more than an incident, or even two or three, with which to make a book. But when I found my plot the story seemed to write itself, and the actors to fit in.

When the development of the Moonta Mine made some of my friends rich they were also liberal. Edward Stirling said that if I wanted a trip to England I should have it at his cost, but it seemed impossible. After the death of Mr. Wren my mother and I went to live with my sister, and put two small incomes together, so as to be able to bring up and educate her two children, a boy and a girl. My brother John had left the railway, and for nine years had been Official Assignee and Curator of Intestate Estates; and in 1863 he had been appointed manager of the new Adelaide branch of the English, Scottish, and Australian Bank. My friend, Mr. Taylor, had helped well to get the position for one he thought the fittest man in the city. He had lost his wife, Miss Mary Ann Dutton when on a visit to England, and at this time was engaged to Miss Harriet McDermott. His sisters both were very cold about the engagement. They did not like second marriages at all, and considered it a disrespect to the first wife's memory, even though a decent interval had elapsed. When he wrote to me about it I took quite a different view. He said it was the kindest and the wisest letter I had ever written in my life, and he knew I had loved his late wife very much. He came to thank me, and to tell me that he had always wished that I should be in England at the time he was there, and that he was going in a P. & 0. boat immediately after his marriage. Although Mr. Stirling had promised to pay my passage, I hesitated about going. There were my mother, who was 72, and my guardianship of the Duvals to think about. I had also undertaken the oversight of old Mrs. Stephens, the widow of one of the early proprietors of The Register. These objections were all overruled. I still hesitated. "I cannot go unless I have money to spend," I urged. "Let me do that," was the generous reply.—"I have left you 500 pounds in my will. Let me have the pleasure of giving you something while I live." I was not too proud to owe that memorable visit to England to my two good friends. John Taylor had put into my hands on board the Goolwa, in which I sailed, a draft for 200 pounds for my spending money, and in the new will he made after his marriage he bequeathed me 300 pounds. I said "Goodby" to him, with good wishes for his health and happiness. I never saw him again. He took a sickly looking child on his knee when crossing the Isthmus of Suez—there was no canal in 1864—to relieve a weary mother. The child had smallpox, and my friend took it and died of it. He was being buried beside his first wife at Brighton when the Goolwa sailed up the Channel after a passage of 14 weeks—as long as that of the Palmyra 25 years before—and the first news we heard was that Miss Taylor had lost a brother, the children a favourite uncle, and I, a friend. It was a sad household, but the Bakewells were in London on business connected with some claims of discovery of the Moonta Mines, and they took me to their house in Palace Gardens. Kensington, till I could arrange to go to my aunt's in Scotland. All our plans about seeing people and places together were, of course, at an end. I was to go "a lone hand." Mrs. Taylor had a posthumous son, who never has set foot in Australia. She married a second time, an English clergyman named Knight, and had several sons, but she has never revisited Adelaide, although she has many relatives here. So the friend who loved Australia, and was eager to do his duty by it—who thoroughly approved of the Hare system of representation, and thought I did well to take it up, was snatched away in the prime of life. I wonder if there is any one alive now to whom his memory is as precious. The Register files may preserve some of his work.

At Palace Gardens the Bakewell family were settled in a furnished house belonging to Col. Palmer, one of the founders of South Australia, though never a resident. Palmer place, North Adelaide, bears his name. Thackeray's house we had to pass when we went out of the street in the direction of the city. His death had occurred in the previous year. I had an engagement with Miss Julia Wedgwood, through an introduction given by Miss Sophia Sinnett, an artist sister of Frederick Sinnett's. I was called for and sent home. I was not introduced to the family. It was a fine large house with men servants and much style. Miss Wedgwood, who was deaf, used an ear trumpet very cleverly. I found her as delightful as Miss Sinnett had represented her to be, and I discovered that Miss Sinnett had been governess to her younger sisters, but that there was real regard for her. I don't know that I ever spent a more delightful evening. She had just had Browning's "Dramatis Personae," and we read together "Rabbi Ben Ezira" and "Prospice." She knew about the Hare scheme of representation, supported by Mill and Fawcett and Craik. She was a good writer, with a fine critical faculty. Everything signed by her name in magazines or reviews was thenceforward interesting to me. I promised her a copy of my "Plea for Pure Democracy," which she accepted and appreciated. By the father's side she was a granddaughter of Josiah Wedgwood, the founder of British pottery as a fine art. Her mother was a daughter of Sir James Mackintosh. Mrs. Wedgwood was so much pleased with my pamphlet that she wanted to be introduced to me, and when I returned to London I had the pleasure of making her acquaintance. Miss Wedgwood gave me a beautifully bound copy of "Men and Women," of which she had a duplicate, which I cherish in remembrance of her.

During my stay I was visited by Mr. Hare. I had to face up to the people I had written to with no idea of any personal communication, and I must confess that I felt I must talk well to retain their good opinion. I promised to pay a visit to the Hares when I came to London for the season. He was a widower with eight children, whom he had educated with the help of a governess, but he was the main factor in their training. The two eldest daughters were married—Mrs. Andrews, the eldest, had helped him in his calculations for his great book on

"Representation." His second daughter was artistic, and was married to John Westlake, an eminent lawyer, great in international law, a pupil of Colenso, who was then in London, and who was the best-abused man in the church. Another visitor was George Cowan, a great friend of my late brother-in-law, Mr. W. J. Wren, who wrote to him till his death, when the pen was taken up by my sister Mary till her death, and then I corresponded with him till his death. He came to London a raw Scotch lad, and met Mr. Wren at the Whittington Club. Both loved books and poetry, and both were struggling to improve themselves on small salaries. George Cowan had been entrusted with the printed slips of "Uphill Work," and had tried it at two publishers without success. I had to delay any operations till I returned to London, and promised to visit the Cowans there.

CHAPTER VII
MELROSE REVISITED

Jack Bakewell and Edward Lancelot Stirling went to see me off by the night train to Dunbar Station, five miles from Thornton-Loch, and I got there in time for breakfast. The old house was just the same except for an oriel window in the drawing room looking out on the North Sea, and the rocks which lay between it and Colhandy path (where my great-grandfather Spence had preached and his wife had preferred Wesley), and Chirnside, or Spence's Mains in the same direction. All the beautiful gardens, the farm village, where about 80 souls lived, the fields and bridges were just as I remembered them. My aunt Margaret was no longer the vigorous business-like woman whom I recollected riding or driving in her little gig an over the farm of 800 English acres which my great-grandfather had rented since 1811. Not the Miss Thompson whom I had introduced into "Uphill Work." She had had a severe stroke of paralysis, and was a prisoner to the house, only being lifted from her bed to be dressed, and to sit in a wheeled chair and be taken round the garden on fine days. The vigorous intellect was somewhat clouded, and the power of speech also; but she retained her memory. She was always at work with her needle (for her hands were not affected) for the London children, grandnieces, and nephews who called her grandmamma, for she had had the care of their Parents during 11 years of her brother Alexander's widowhood. But Aunt Margaret could play a capital game of whist—long whist. I could see that she missed it much on Sunday. It was her only relaxation. She had given up the farm to James Brodie, who had married her cousin Jane, the eldest of the two children she had mothered, and he had to come to the farm once or twice a week, having a still larger farm of his own in East Lothian, and a stock farm in Berwickshire also to look after. The son of the old farm steward, John Burnet, was James Brodie's steward, and I think the farm was well managed, but not so profitable as in old times. Aunt Mary said, in her own characteristic way, "she always knew that her sister was a clever woman, but that the cleverest thing she had done was taking up farming and carrying it on for 30 years when it was profitable, and turning it over when it began to fall off." But she turned it over handsomely, and did not interfere in the management. My Aunt Mary deserves a chapter for herself. She was my beau ideal of what a maiden aunt should be, though why she was never married puzzles more than me. Between my mother and her there was a love passing the love of sisters—my father liked her better than his own sisters. When my letter announcing my probable visit reached her she misread it, and thought it was Helen herself who was to come; and when she found out her mistake she shed many tears. I was all very well in my way, but I was not Helen. It was not the practice in old times to blazon an engagement, or to tell of an offer that had been declined; but my mother firmly believed that her sister Mary, the cleverest and, as she thought, the handsomest of the five sisters, had never in her life had an offer of marriage, although she had a love disappointment at 30. She had fixed her affections on a brilliant but not really worthy man, and she had to tear him out of her heart with considerable difficulty. It cost her a severe illness, out of which she emerged with what she believed to be a change of heart. She was a converted Christian. I myself don't think there was so much change. She was always a noble, generous woman, but she found great happiness in religion. Aunt Mary's disappointment made her most sympathetic to all love stories, and without any disappointment at all, I think I may say the same of myself. She was very popular with the young friends of her youngest brother, who might have experienced calf love; so very real, but so very ineffectual. One of these said to her:—"Oh, Miss Mary, you're just a delight, you are so witty." Another, when she spoke of some man who talked such delightful nonsense, said, "If you would only come to Branxholme I'd talk nonsense to you the haill (whole) day."

When I arrived at the old home I found Aunt Mary vigorously rubbing her hand and wrist (she had slipped downstairs in a neighbour's house, and broken her arm, and had to drive home before she could have it set). No one from the neighbour's house went to accompany her; no one came to enquire; no message was sent. When she recovered so far as to be able to be out, she met at Dunbar the gentleman and lady also driving in their conveyance. They greeted each other, and aunt could not resist the temptation to say:—"I am so glad to see you, and so glad that you have spoken to me, for I thought you were so offended at my taking the liberty of breaking my arm in your house that you did not mean to speak to me again." This little expression of what the French call malice, not the English meaning, was the only instance I can recollect of Aunt Mary's not putting the kindest construction on everybody's words and actions. But when I think of the love that Aunt Mary gathered to herself from brothers, sisters, nephews, nieces, cousins, and friends—it seems as if the happiest wife and mother of a large family could not reckon up as rich stores of affection. She was the unfailing correspondent of those members of the family who were separated by land and ocean from the old home, the link that often bound these together, the most tolerant to their failings, the most liberal in her aid—full of suggestions, as well as of sympathy. Now, in my Aunt Margaret's enfeebled state, she was the head of the house and the director of all things. Although she had differed from the then two single sisters and the family generally at the time of the disruption of the Church of Scotland, and gone over to the Free Church, the more intensely Calvinistic of the two, though accepting the same standards—the Westminster Confession and the Shorter Catechism—all the harsher features fell off the living texture of her faith like cold water off a duck's back. From natural preference she chose for her devotions those parts of the Bible which I selected with deliberate intention. She wondered to find so much spiritual kinship with me, when I built on such a different foundation. When I suggested that the 109th Psalm, which she read as the allotted portion in "Fletcher's Family Devotions," was not fit to be read in a Christian household, she said meekly—"You are quite right, I shall mark it, and never read it again."

My mother always thought me like her sister Mary, and when I asked Mr. Taylor if he saw any resemblance between us, he said, with cruel candour—"Oh, no. Your Aunt Mary is a very handsome woman." But in ways and manners, both my sister Mary and myself had considerable resemblances to our mother's favourite sister; and I can see traces of it in my own nieces. There can be no direct descent from maiden aunts, though the working ants and bees do not inherit their industrious habits from either male or female parents, but from their maiden aunts. Galton's theory, that potentialities not utilized by individuals or by their direct descendants may miss a generation or two, opens a wide field of thought, and collaterals may draw from the original source what was never suspected. And the Brodies intermarried in such a way as to shock modern ideas. When my father was asked if a certain Mr. Dudgeon, of Leith, was related to him, he said—"He is my mother's cousin and my stepmother's cousin, and my father-in-law's cousin, and my mother-in-law's cousin." Except for Spences and Wauchopes there was not a relative of my father that was not related to my mother. Grandfather Brodie married his cousin, and Grandfather Spence married his late wife, Janet Parks cousin Katherine Swanston. I cannot see that these close marriages produced degenerates, either physical or mental, in the case of my own family.

Of the twelve months I spent in the old country, I spent six with the dear old aunts. How proud Aunt Mary was of my third novel, with the sketch of Aunt Margaret in it, of the Cornhill article, and the request from Mr. Wilson to write for The Fortnightly. I introduced her to new books and especially to new poets; she had never heard of Browning and Jean Ingelow. She was so much cleverer than her neighbours that I often wondered how she could put up with them. How conservative these farmers and farmers' wives and daughters were, to be sure. These big tenants considered themselves quite superior to tradesmen, even to merchants, unless they were in a big way. There was infinitely more difference between their standard of living and that of their labourers than between theirs and that of the aristocratic landlords. James Barnet, the farm steward, said to me—"you have brought down the price of wheat with your Australian grain, and you do big things in wool, but you can never touch us in meat." This was quite true in 1865. I expected to see some improvement in the farm hamlet, but the houses built by the landlord were still very poor and bare. The wages had risen a little since 1839, but not much. The wheaten loaf was cheaper, and so was tea and sugar, but the poor were still living on porridge and bannocks of barley and pease meal instead of tea and white bread. It was questionable if they were as well nourished. There were 100 souls living on the farms of Thornton and Thornton Loch.

A short visit from Mrs. Graham to me at Thornton Loch opened up to Aunt Mary some of my treasures of memory. She asked me to recite "Brother in the Lane," Hood's "Tale of a Trumpet," "Locksley Hall." "The Pied Piper," and Jean Ingelow's "Songs of Seven." She made me promise to go to see her, and find out how much she had to do for her magnificent salary of 30 pounds a year; but she impressed Aunt Mary much. Mrs. Graham had found that the Kirkbeen folks, among whom she lived, were more impressed by the six months' experiences of two maiden ladies, who had gone to Valparaiso to join a brother who died, than with her fresh and racy descriptions of four young Australian colonies. She had seen Melbourne from 1852 to 1855—a wonderful growth and development. The only idea the ladies from Valparaiso formed about Australia was that it was hot and must be Roman Catholic, and consequently the Sabbath must be desecrated. It was in vain that my friend spoke of the Scots Church and Dr. Cairns's Church. Heat and Roman Catholicism were inseparably connected in their minds.

Visiting Uncle and Aunt Handyside and grown-up cousins, whom I left children, I saw a lot of good farming and the easy circumstances which I always associated with tenants' holdings in East Lothian. Next farm to Fenton was Fentonbarns, a Show place, which was held by George Hope, a cousin of my grandmother's He was an exceptional man—a radical, a freetrader, and a Unitarian. Cobden died that year. Uncle Handyside was surprised that George Hope did not go into mourning for him. John Bright still lived, and he was the bete noire of the Conservatives in that era; and the abolition of the corn laws was held to be the cause of the agricultural distress—not the high rent of agricultural land. George Hope was a striking personality. When my friend J. C. Woods was minister at St. Mark's Unitarian Church, Edinburgh, Mr. Hope used to be called the Bishop, though he lived 16 miles off. When the first Mrs. Woods died, leaving an infant son, it was Mrs. Hope who cared for it till it could go to his relatives in Ireland. Later he stood for Parliament himself. In the paper I wrote over the name of Edward Wilson for The Fortnightly I noted how the House of Commons represented the people—or misrepresented them. The House consisted of peers and sons of peers, military and naval officers, bankers, brewers, and landownership was represented enormously, but there were only two tenant farmers in the House. It was years after my return to Australia that I heard of his unsuccessful candidature, and that when he sought to take another lease of Fentonbarns, he was told that under no circumstances would his offer be entertained. Fentonbarns had been farmed by, three generations of Hopes for 100 years, and to no owner by parchment titles could it have been more dear. George Hope's friend, Russell, of The Scotsman, fulminated against the injustice of refusing a lease to the foremost agriculturist in Scotland—and when you say that you may say of the United Kingdom—because the tenant held certain political opinions and had the courage to express them. My uncle Handyside, however, always maintained that his neighbour was the most honourable man in business that he knew, and far from being an atheist or even a deist, he had family prayers, and on the occasion of a death in the family, the funeral service was most impressive. He was one of the salt of the earth, and the atmosphere was clearer around him for his presence.

But I must give some space to my visit to Melrose, my childhood's home. My father's half-sister Janet Reid was alive and though her two sons were, one at St. Kitts and the other at Grand Canary, she lived with an old husband and her only daughter in Melrose still.. I can never forget the look of tender pity cast on me as I was sitting in our old seat in church, looking at seats filled by another generation. The paterfamilias, so wonderfully like his father of 1839, and sons and daughters, sitting in the place of uncles and aunts settled elsewhere. They grieved that I had been banished from the romantic associations and the high civilization of Melrose to rough it in the wilds, while my heart was full of thankfulness that I had moved to the wider spaces and the more varied activities of a new and progressive colony. My dear old teacher was still alive, though the school had been closed for many years. She lived at St. Mary's with her elder sister, who had taught me sewing and had done the housekeeping, but she herself was almost blind, and a girl came every day to read to her for two or three hours. She told me what a good thing it was that she knew all the Psalms in the prose version by heart, for in the sleepless nights which accompany old age so often they were such a comfort to her in the night watches. I had sent her my two novels when they were published, "Clara Morison" and "Tender and True." She would have been glad if they had been more distinctly religious in tone. Indeed, the novel I began at 19 would have suited her better, but my brother's insistence on reading it every day as I wrote it somehow made me see what poor stuff it was, and I did not go far with it. But Miss Phin was, on the whole, pleased with my progress, and glad that I was able to go to see her and talk of old times. How very small the village of Melrose looked! How little changed! The distances to the neighbouring villages of Darnick and Newstead, and across the Tweed to Gattonsville, seemed so shrunken. It was not so far to Abbotsford as to Norwood. The very Golden Hills looked lower than my childish recollection of them. Aunt Janet Reid rejoiced over me sufficiently. "You are not like your mother in the face, but, oh, Katie, you are like dear Mrs. David in your ways. How I was determined to hate her when she came to Melrose first. I was not 13 and she was taking away the best of my brothers, the one that I liked best; but it did not take long before I was as fond of her as of David himself."

I also had the pleasure of visiting Mr. Murray, the parish schoolmaster, who taught my three brothers, then retired, living with his daughter, Louisa, an old schoolfellow at Miss Phin's. There was an absurd idea current in 1865 that all visiting Australians were rich and I could not disabuse people of that notion. Of all the two families of Brodies and Spences who came out in 1839 there was only my brother John who could be called successful. He was then manager of the Adelaide branch of the English, Scottish, and Australian Bank. If it had not been for help from the wonderful aunts from time to time both families would have been stranded. I had the greatest faith in the future of Australia, but I felt that for such gifts as I possessed there was no market at home. Possibly I should have tried literature earlier if I had remained in Scotland, but I am not at all sure that I could have succeeded as well. For the first time in my life I had as much money as I wanted. I am surprised now that I spent that 200 pounds when I had so much hospitality. In fact, except for a week in Paris, I never had any hotel expenses. I had got the money to enjoy it and I did. This was what my friend wished. I made a few presents. I bought some to take home with me. I spent money on dress freely, so as to present a proper appearance when visiting. I was liberal with veils, though I hate the practice. To a woman who had to look on both sides of a shilling since 1839 this experience was new and delightful. Among other people I went to see was Mrs. C——. the widow of the Tory writer and branch bank manager, who was my father's successful rival. He was not speculative like my father. He was a keen business man and had a great hunger for land.

On the gravestones around Melrose Abbey are many names with the avocation added—John Smith, builder; William Hogg, mason—but many with the word portioner. They were small proprietors, but they were not distinguished for the careful cultivation which in France is known as "LA PETITE CULTURE." No; the portions were most carelessly handled, and in almost every instance they were "bonded" or mortgaged. I recollect in old days these portioners used to make moonlight, flittings and disappear, or they sold off their holdings openly and went to America, meaning the United States. The tendency was to buy up these portions, and a considerable estate could be built up by any shrewd man who had money, or the command of it. Before we left Melrose in 1839, Mr. C—— had possession of a good deal of land. When he died he left property of the value of 90,000 pounds, an unheard-of estate for a country writer before the era of freetrade and general expansion. He had asked so much revenue from the railway company when the plan was to cut through the gardens we as children used to play in, that the company made a deviation and left the garden severely alone. The eldest daughter had married a landed proprietor, the second was single, the third married to a wealthy man in the west, the fourth the richest widow in Scotland. One son had land, and the other son land, and another business training. All was material success, and I am sure I did not grudge it to them, but when I took stock of real things I had not the least glimmering of a wish to exchange. One generally desires a little more money than one has; but even that may cost too much. I think my dear old Aunt Reid felt that the Spences had gone down in my father's terrible smash in 1839, and the C—— family had steadily gone up, and she was pleased that a niece from Australia, who had written two books and a wonderful pamphlet, and, more important still in the eyes of Mrs. Grundy, had money to spend and to give, was staying with her in Melrose, and wearing good and well made clothes. Old servants—the old laundress—old schoolfellows were visited. My father's old clerk, Allan Freer, had a good business in Melrose, though not equal to that of the Tory firm. I think the portioners were all sold out before he could enter the field, and the fate of these Melrose people has thoroughly emphasized for me the importance of having our South Australian workmen's blocks, the glory of Mr. Cotton's life, maintained always on the same footing of perpetual lease dependent on residence. If the small owner has the freehold, he is tempted to mortgage it, and then in most instances the land is lost to him, and added to the possessions of the man who has money. With a perpetual lease, there is the same security of tenure as in the freehold—indeed, there is more security, because he cannot mortgage. I did not see the land question as clearly on this 1865 visit, as I did later; but the extinction of the old portioners and the wealth acquired by the moneyed man of Melrose gave me cause for thinking.

CHAPTER VIII
I VISIT EDINBURGH AND LONDON

A visit to Glasgow and to the relatives of my sister-in-law opened out a different vista to me. This was a great manufacturing and commercial city, which had far outgrown Edinburgh in population and wealth; but the Edinburgh people still boasted of being the Athens of the north, the ancient capital with the grandest historic associations. In Glasgow I fell in with David Murray and his wife (of D. & W. Murray Adelaide)—not quite so important a personage as be became later. Not a relative of mine; but a family connection, for his brother William married Helen Cumming, Mrs. J. B. Spence's sister. David Murray was always a great collector of paintings, and especially of prints, which last he left to the Adelaide Art Gallery. He was a close friend of my brother John's until the death of the latter. One always enjoys meeting with Adelaide people in other lands, and comparing the most recent items of news. I went to Dumfries according to promise, and spent many days with my old friend Mrs. Graham, but stayed the night always with her sister, Mrs. Maxwell, wife of a printer and bookseller in the town. Dumfries was full of Burns's relies and memorials. Mr. Gilfillan had taken the likeness of Mrs. Burns and her granddaughter when he was a young man, and Mrs. Maxwell corresponded with the granddaughter. It was also full of associations with Carlyle. His youngest sister, Jean the Craw, as she was called on account of her dark hair and complexion was Mrs. Aitkin, a neighbour and close friend of Mrs. Maxwell. I was taken to see her, and I suppose introduced as a sort of author, and she regretted much that this summer Tom was not coming to visit her at Dumfries. She was a brisk, cheery person, with some clever daughters, who were friends of the Maxwell girls. When the Froude memorials came out no one was more indignant than Jean the Craw—"Tom and his wife always understood each other. They were not unhappy, though after her death he reproached himself for some things."

I found that my friend had just as much to do from morning to night as she could do, and I hoped with a great hope that "Uphill Work" would be published, and all the world would see how badly capable and industrious women were paid. I fancied that a three-volume novel would be read, marked, and inwardly digested by everybody! But Mrs. Graham was appreciated by the matron, the doctors, and by the people of Dumfries, as she had not been in the village of Kirkbeen. Her picturesque descriptions of life in the various colonies interested home-staying folk, for she had the keenest observing faculties. There was an old cousin of Uncle Handyside's who always turned the conversation on to Russia, where he had visited successful brothers; but his talk was not incisive. My cousin Agnes asked me when I supposed this visit was paid, and I said a few years ago, probably, when she laughed and said—"Nicol Handyside spent six weeks in Russia 30 years ago, and he has been talking about it ever since." One visit I paid in Edinburgh to an old lady from Melrose, who lived with a married daughter. She had always been very deaf, and the daughter was out. With great difficulty I got her to see by my card that my name was Spence. "Are you Jessie Spence?" I shook my head. "No; Katie." "Are you Mary Spence?" Another headshake, "No; I am Katie." "Then who are you?" She could understand the negative by the headshaking, but not anything else. I wanted a piece of paper or a slate badly, but the daughter came in and made her mother understand that I was the middle Spence girl, and then the old lady said, "It is a very hot country you come from," her only idea apparently of wonderful Australia. And to think that in times long past some intriguing aunts tried very hard to arrange a marriage between my father and the deaf young lady who had about 600 pounds a year in land in and near Melrose. She might have been my mother! The idea was appalling! None of her children inherited the deafness, and they took a fair proportion of good looks from their father, for the mother was exceedingly homely. A brightlooking grandson was on the rug looking through a bound volume of Punch, as my nephew in Australia loved to do. The two mothers were school companions and playmates.

My return to London introduced me to a wider range of society. I had admissions to the Ladies' Gallery of the House of Commons from Sir Charles Dilke, Professor Pearson's friend, and I had invitations to stay for longer or shorter periods with people various in means, in tastes, and in interests. To Mr. Hare I was especially drawn, and I should have liked to join him and his family in their yearly walking tour, which was to be through the Tyrol and Venice; but Aunt Mary protested for two good and sufficient reasons. The first was that I could not walk 16 or 20 miles a day, even in the mountains, which Katie Hare said was so much easier than on the plains; and the second was that to take six weeks out of my visit to the old country was a great deal too much. If it could have done any good to proportional representation I might have stood out; but it could not. For that I have since travelled thousands of miles by sea and by land; and, though not on foot, I have undergone much bodily fatigue and mental strain, but in these early days of the movement it had only entered the academic stage. My "Plea for Pure Democracy" had been written at a white heat of enthusiasm. I do not think I ever before or since reached a higher level. I took this reform more boldly than Mr. Mill, who sought by giving extra votes for property and university degrees or learned professions to cheek the too great advance of democracy. I was prepared to trust the people; and Mr. Hare was also confident that, if all the people were equitably represented in Parliament, the good would be stronger than the evil. The wise would be more effectual than the foolish. I do not think any one whom I met took the matter up so passionately as I did; and I had a feeling that in our new colonies the reform would meet with less obstruction than in old countries bound by precedent and prejudiced by vested interests. Parliament was the preserve of the wealthy in the United Kingdom. There was no property qualification for the candidate in South Australia, and we had manhood suffrage.

South Australia was the first community to give the secret ballot for political elections. It had dispensed with Grand Juries. It had not required a member of either House to stand a new election if he accepted Ministerial office. Every elected man was eligible for office. South Australia had been founded by doctrinaires, and occasionally a cheap sneer had been levelled at it on that account; but, to my mind, that was better than the haphazard way in which other colonies grew. When I visited Sir Rowland Hill he was recognised as the great post office reformer. To me he was also one of the founders of our province, and the first pioneer of quota representation. When I met Matthew Davenport Hill I respected him because he tried to keep delinquent boys out of gaol, and promoted the establishment of reform schools; but I also was grateful to him for suggesting to his brother the park lands which surround Adelaide, and give us both beauty and health. To Col. Light, who laid out the city so well, we owe the many open spaces and squares; but he did not originate the idea of the park lands. Much of the work of Mr. Davenport Hill and of his brother Frederick I took up later with their niece (Miss C. E. Clark), and their ideas have been probably more thoroughly carried out in South Australia than anywhere else; but in 1865 I was learning a great deal that bore fruit afterwards.

I fear it would make this narrative too long if I went into detail about the interesting people I met. Florence and Rossamund Davenport Hill introduced me to Miss Frances Power Cobbe, whose "Intuitive Morals" I admired so much. At Sir Rowland Hill's I met Sir Walter Crofter, a prison reformer; Mr. Wells, Editor of "All the Year Round;" Charles Knight, who had done so much for good and cheap literature; Madame Bodichon (formerly Barbara Smith), the great friend and correspondent of George Eliot, who was interesting to me because by introducing the Australian eucalyptus to Algeria she had made an unhealthy marshy country quite salubrious. She had a salon, where I met very clever men and women—English and French—and which made me wish for such things in Adelaide. The kindness and hospitality that were shown to me—an absolute stranger—by all sorts of people were surprising. Mr. and Mrs. Westlake took me on Sunday to see Bishop Colenso. He showed me the photo of the enquiring Zulu who made him doubt the literal truth of the early books of the Bible, and presented me with the people's edition of his work on the Pentateuch.

In all my travels and visits I saw little of the theatre or concert room, and some of the candid confessions of Mrs. Oliphant might stand for my own. I had read so many plays before I saw one that the unreality of much of the acted drama impressed me unfavourably. The asides in particular seemed impossible, and I think the more carefully the pieces are put on the stage the more critical I become concerning their probability; and when I hear the praise of the beautiful and expensive theatrical wardrobes which, in the case of actresses seem to set the fashion for the wealthy and well-born, I feel that it is a costly means of making the story more unlikely. I seem to lose the identity of the heroine who in two hours wears three or four different toilettes complete. As Mrs. Oliphant did not identify the "nobody in white tights" who rendered from "Twelfth Night" the lovely lines beginning "That strain again; it had a dying fall" with the Orsino she had imagined when reading the play, so I, who knew "She Stoops to Conquer" almost by heart, was disappointed when I saw it on the stage. I was taken to the opera once by Mr. and Mrs. Bakewell, and heard Patti in "Don Giovanni," at Covent Garden, but opera of all kinds is wasted on me. I liked some of the familiar airs and choruses, but all opera needs far more make-believe than I am capable of. It is a pity that I am so insensible to the youngest and the most progressive of the fine arts. I am, however, in the good company of Mrs. Oliphant, who, speaking of the musical parties in Eton, where she lived so long, for the education of tier boys, writes in words that suit me perfectly: "In one of these friends' houses a family quartet played what were rather new and terrible to me— long sonatas and concerted pieces which filled my soul with dismay. It is a dreadful confession to make, and proceeds from want of education and instruction, but I fear any appreciation of music I have is purely literary. I love a song and a 'tune;' the humblest fiddler has sometimes given me the greatest pleasure, and sometimes gone to my heart; but music, properly so called, the only music that many of my friends would listen to, is to me a wonder and a mystery. My mind wanders through adagios and andantes, gaping, longing to understand. Will no one tell me what it means? I want to find the old unhappy far off things which Wordsworth imagined in the Gaelic song of the 'Highland Lass.' I feel out of it, uneasy, thinking all the time what a poor creature I must be. I remember the mother of the sonata players approaching me with beaming countenance on the occasion of one of these performances, expecting the compliment which I faltered forth, doing my best not to look insincere. 'And I have this every evening of my life,' cried the triumphant mother. 'Good heavens, and you have survived it all' was my internal response." But the worst thing is when you do not expect a musical evening and this superior music is sprung on you. Mrs. Webster and I were once invited to meet some very interesting people, some of the best conversationalists in Melbourne, and we were given high-class music instead, and scarcely could a remark be exchanged when a warning finger was held up and silence insisted on. I could not sing, but sometimes I attempted to hum a tune. I recollect during my first visit to Melbourne, my little nephew Johnnie, delighted in the rhymes and poems which I recited; but one day when I was ironing I began to sing, and he burst out with "Don't sing, auntie; let me hear the voice of your words." So for my own delectation I began Wordsworth's "Leechgatherer"—

> There was a roaring in the wind all night,
>
> The rain came heavily and fell in floods;
>
> But now the sun is rising calm and bright.
>
> The birds are singing in the distant woods;
>
> Over his own sweet voice the stock dove broods.
>
> The jay makes answer as the magpie chatters,
>
> And all the air is filled with pleasant noise of waters.

"Oh, that's pretty, auntie; say it again," I said it again, and yet again, at his request, till he could almost repeat it. And he was not quite 4 years old. He is still alive, and has not become a poet, which was what I expected in those early days. He could repeat great screeds of Browning's "Pied Piper of Hamelin," which was his especial favourite. Music has often cheated me of what is to me the keenest pleasure in life. Like Samuel Johnson, I enjoy greatly "good talk," though I never took such a dominant part in it. There are two kinds of people who reduce me to something like silence—those who know too little and those who know too much. My brother-in-law's friend, Mr. Cowan, was a great talker, and a good one, but he scarcely allowed me a fair share. He was also an admirable correspondent.

One predominant talker I met at Mr. Edwin Hill's— William Ellis, a special friend of the Hills, and a noteworthy man. One needs to look back 60 years to become conscious of how much English education was in the hands of the church. Not only the public schools and the university were overshadowed by the Established Church, but what schools were accessible to the poor were a sort of appanage to the rectory, and the teachers were bound to work for the good of the church and the convenience of the incumbent. The commercial schools, which were independent of the church, to which Non-conformists sent their boys, were satirised by Dickens, and they deserved the satire. The masters were generally incompetent, and the assistant teachers or ushers were the most miserable in regard to payment and status. William Ellis expended large sums of money, and almost all his leisure, in establishing secular schools that were good for something. He called them Birkbeck schools, thus doing honour to the founder of mechanics' institutes, and perhaps the founder of the first of these schools; and he taught what he called social science in them himself. He was the Senor Ferrer of England; and, though he escaped martyrdom in the more enlightened country he was looked on suspiciously by those who considered education that was not founded on revealed religion and permeated by its doctrines as dangerous and revolutionary.

But there was one great personage who saw the value of those teachings on things that make for human happiness and intellectual freedom, and that was the Prince Consort. He asked William Ellis to give some lessons to the eldest of the Royal children—the Princess Victoria, Prince Edward (our present King), and Prince Alfred, afterwards Duke of Saxe-Coburg. Mr. Ellis said all three were intelligent, and Princess Victoria exceptionally so. What a tragedy it was—more so than that of many an epic or drama—that the Princess Royal and the husband of her choice, who had educated themselves and each other to take the reins of the German Empire, and had drawn up so many Plans for the betterment of the general conditions of the people, should, on their accession to power, have met death standing on the steps of the throne; and that only a powerless widow should have been left without much authority over her masterful son. But my firm belief is that in many of the excellent things that the Kaiser William has done for his people, he is working on the plans that had been committed to writing by the Crown Prince and Princess. Her father's memory was so dear to the Crown Princess that anything he had suggested to her was cherished all her life; and I do not doubt that these early lessons on the right relation of human beings to each other—the social science which regards human happiness as depending on justice and toleration—is even now bearing fruit in the Fatherland. Shortsighted mortals see the immediate failures, but in the larger eye of the Infinite and the Eternal there is always progress towards better things from every honest attempt to remedy injustice, and to increase knowledge.

I arranged for a week in Paris with my young friends, Rosa and Symonds Clark, of Hazelwood, and we travelled as far as Paris with the Hare family, who went on to the Tyrol. We enjoyed the week. Louis Napoleon appeared then to be quite secure on his throne, and we saw the fetes and illuminations for his birthday. What a day and night of rain it was! But the thousands of people, joyful and good-humoured under umbrellas or without them—gave us a favourable impression of Parisian crowds. In London I had been with Mr. Cowan in the crush to the theatre. It was contrary to his principles to book seats, and I never was so frightened in my life. I thought a London crowd rough and merciless. I was the only one of the party who could speak any French, and I spoke it badly, and had great difficulty in following French conversations; but we got into a hotel where no English was spoken, and managed to pull through. But we did not know a soul, and I think we did not learn so much from our week's sightseeing as we should have done if Miss Katie Hare had stayed the week with us.

I then paid a visit to Birmingham, and spent a week at the sittings of the British Association. By subscribing a guinea I was made an Associate, and some of the sessions were very interesting, but much too deep for me. I sat out a lecture on the Higher Mathematics, by Professor Henry Smith, to whom Professor Pearson gave me an introduction, in hopes that I might visit Oxford; but he was going abroad, and I could not go to Oxford if I knew nobody—especially alone. I went, however, to Carr's Lane Chapel, where a humble friend had begged me to go, because there she had been converted, and there the Rev. R. W. Dale happened to preach on "Where prayer was wont to be made." He said that consecration was not due to a Bishop or to any ecclesiastical ceremony, but to the devout prayers and praise of the faithful souls within it—that thousands over Scotland and England, and others in America, Australia, and New Zealand, look back to words which they had heard and praises and prayers in which they had joined as the holiest times in their lives. I thought of my good Mrs. Ludlow, and thanked God for her. When Mr. Cowan took me to the church in Essex place where he and his friend Wren used to hear Mr. W. J. Fox, M.P. for Oldham, preach, a stranger, a young American, was there. I found out afterwards he was Moncure Conway, and he gave us a most striking discourse. There was going on in Birmingham at this time a controversy between the old Unitarians and the new. In the Church of the Messiah the old ministers gave a series of sermons on the absolute truth of the New Testament miracles. The Old Testament he was quite willing to give up, but he pinned his faith on those wrought by Christ and His apostles. Some of the congregation told me they had never thought of doubting them before, but the more Mr. B. defended them as the bulwarks of Christianity, the more they felt that our religion rested on other foundations. I saw a good deal of the industrial life of Birmingham, and had a sight of the Black Country by day and by night. Joseph Chamberlain was then a young man; I believe he was a Sunday school teacher. The Unitarian Sunday Schools taught writing and arithmetic as well as reading. In the terrible lack of national day schools many of the poor had no teaching at all but what was given on Sundays, and no time on other days of the week to learn anything. I could not help contrasting the provision made by the parish schools of Scotland out of the beggarly funds or tithes given for church and schools out of the spoils of the Ancient Church by the Lords of the Congregation. Education was not free, but it was cheap, and it was general. Scotchmen made their way all over the world better than Englishmen mainly because they were better educated. The Sunday school was not so much needed, and was much later in establishing itself in Scotland. Good Hannah More taught girls to read the Bible under a spreading tree in her garden because no church would give her a place to teach in. "If girls were taught to read where would we get servants?" It was an early cry.

CHAPTER IX
MEETING WITH J. S. MILL AND GEORGE ELIOT

I leave to the last of my experiences in the old world in 1865-6 my interviews with John Stuart Mill and George Eliot. Stuart Mill's wife was the sister of Arthur and of Alfred Hardy, of Adelaide, and the former had given to me a copy of the first edition of Mill's "Political Economy," with the original dedication to Mrs. John Taylor, who afterwards became Mill's wife, which did not appear in subsequent editions; but, as he had two gift copies of the same edition, Mr. Hardy sent it on to me with his almost illegible handwriting:—"To Miss Spence from the author, not, indeed, directly, but in the confidence felt by the presenter that in so doing he is fulfilling the wish of the author—viz., circulating his opinions, more especially in such quarters as the present, where they will be accurately considered and tested." I had also seen the dedication to Harriet Mill's beloved memory of the noble book on "Liberty." Of her own individual work there was only one specimen extant—an article on the "Enfranchisement of women," included in Mill's collected essays—very good, certainly, but not so overpoweringly excellent as I expected. Of course, it was an early advocacy of the rights of women, or rather a revival of Mary Wollstoneeraft's grand vindication of the rights of the sex; and this was a reform which Mill himself took up more warmly than proportional representation, and advocated for years before Mr. Hare's revelation. For myself, I considered electoral reform on the Hare system of more value than the enfranchisement of women, and was not eager for the doubling of the electors in number, especially as the new voters would probably be more ignorant and more apathetic than the old. I was accounted a weak-kneed sister by those who worked primarily for woman suffrage, although I was as much convinced as they were that I was entitled to a vote, and hoped that I might be able to exercise it before I was too feeble to hobble to the poll. I have unfortunately lost the letter Mr. Mill wrote to me about my letters to The Register, and my "Plea for Pure Democracy," but it gave him great pleasure to see that a new idea both of the theory and practice of politics had been taken up and expanded by a woman, and one from that Australian colony, of which he had watched and aided the beginnings, as is seen by the name of Mill terrace, North Adelaide, to-day. Indeed, both Hare and Mill told me their first converts were women; and I felt that the absolute disinterestedness of my "Plea," which was not for myself, but only that the men who were supposed to represent me at the polling booth should be equitably represented themselves, lent weight to my arguments. I have no axe to grind— no political party to serve; so that it was not until the movement for the enfranchisement of women grew too strong to be neglected that I took hold of it at all; and I do not claim any credit for its success in South Australia and the Commonwealth, further than this—that by my writings and my spoken addresses I showed that one woman had a steady grasp on politics and on sociology. In 1865, when I was in England, Mr. Mill was permanently resident at Avignon, where his wife died, but he had to come to England to canvass for a seat in Parliament for Westminster as an Independent member, believed at that time to be an advanced Radical, but known to be a philosopher, and an economist of the highest rank in English literature. I had only one opportunity of seeing him personally, and I did not get so much out of him as I expected—he was so eager to know how the colony and colonial people were developing. He asked me about property in land and taxation, and the relations between employers and employes, and I was a little amused and a little alarmed when he said he was glad to get information from such a good authority. I had to disclaim such knowledge; but he said he knew I was observant and thoughtful, and what I had seen I had seen well. He was particularly earnest about woman's suffrage, and Miss Taylor, his stepdaughter, said she thought he had made a mistake in asking for the vote for single women only and widows with property and wives who had a separate estate; it would have been more logical to have asked for the vote on the same terms as were extended to men. The great man said meekly—"Well, perhaps I have made a mistake, but I thought with a property qualification the beginning would awake less antagonism." He said to me that if I was not to return to London till January we were not likely to meet again. He walked with me bareheaded to the gate, and it was farewell for both.

Wise man as Mill was he did not foresee that his greatest object, the enfranchisement of women, would be carried at the antipodes long before there was victory either in England or America. When I received, in 1869 from the publisher, Mr. Mill's last book, "The Subjection of Women," I wrote thanking him for the gift. The reply was as follows:—"Avignon, November 28, 1869—Dear Madam—Your letter of August 16 has been sent to me here. The copy of my little book was intended for you, and I had much pleasure in offering it. The movement against women's disabilities generally, and for the suffrage in particular, has made great progress in England since you were last there. It is likely, I think, to be successful in the colonies later than in England, because the want of equality in social advantages between women and men is less felt in the colonies owing, perhaps, to women's having less need of other occupations than those of married life—I am, dear Madam, yours very truly, J. S. Mill." I have always held that, though the Pilgrim Fathers ignored the right of the Pilgrim Mothers to the credit of founding the American States—although these women had to take their full share of the toils and hardships and perils of pioneer and frontier life, and had in addition to put up with the Pilgrim Fathers themselves—Australian colonization was carried out by men who were conscious of the service of their helpmates, and grateful for it. In New Zealand and South Australia, founded on the Wakefield system, where the sexes were almost equal in number, and the immigration was mainly that of families, the first great triumphs for the political enfranchisement of women were won, and through South Australia the women of the Commonwealth obtained the Federal vote for both Houses: whereas even in the sparsely inhabited western states in the United States which have obtained the State vote the Federal vote is withheld from them. But Mill died in 1873, 20 years before New Zealand or Colorado obtained woman's suffrage.

In treating of my one interview with Mr. Mill I have carried the narrative down to 1869. With regard to my single meeting with George Eliot, I have to begin in 1865, and conclude even later. Before I left England Mr. Williams, of Smith, Elder, & Co., offered me an introduction to George Henry Lewes, and I expressed the hope that it might also include an introduction to George Eliot, whose works I so admired. Mr. Lewes being away from home when I called, I requested that the introductory letter of Mr. Williams should be taken to George Eliot herself. She received me in the big Priory drawing room, with the grand piano, where she held her receptions and musical evenings; but she asked me if I had any business relating to the article which Mr. Williams had mentioned, and I had to confess that I had none. For once I felt myself at fault. I did not get on with George Eliot. She said she was not well, and she did not look well. That strong pale face, where the features were those of Dante or Savanarola, did not soften as Mill's had done. The voice, which was singularly musical and impressive, touched me—I am more susceptible to voices than to features or complexion—but no subject that I started seemed to fall in with her ideas, and she started none in which I could follow her lead pleasantly. It was a short interview, and it was a failure. I felt I had been looked on as an inquisitive Australian desiring an interview upon any pretext; and indeed, next day I had a letter from Mr. Williams, in which he told me that, but for the idea that I had some business arrangement to speak of, she would not have seen me at all. So I wrote to Mr. Williams that, as I had been received by mistake, I should never mention the interview; but that impertinent curiosity was not at all my motive in going that unlucky day to The Priory.

Years passed by. I read everything, poetry and prose, that came from George Eliot's pen, and was so strong an admirer of her that Mr. W. L. Whitham, who took charge of the Unitarian Church while our pastor (Mr. Woods) had a long furlough in England, asked me to lecture on her works to his Mutual Improvement Society, and I undertook the task with joy. Mr. H. G. Turner asked for the MS. to publish in the second number of The Melbourne Review, a very promising quarterly for politics and literature. I thought that, if I sent the review to George Eliot with a note it might clear me from the suspicion of being a mere vulgar lionhunter. Her answer was as follows:—"The Priory,

North Bank, Regent's Park, September 4, 1876. Dear Madam—Owing to an absence of some months, it was only the other day that I read your kind letter of April 17; and, although I have long been obliged to give up answering the majority of letters addressed to me, I felt much pleased that you had given me an opportunity of answering one from you; for I have always remembered your visit with a regretful feeling that I had probably caused you some pain by a rather unwise effort to give you a reception which the state of my health at the moment made altogether blundering and infelicitous. The mistake was all on my side, and you were not in the least to blame. I also remember that your studies have been of a serious kind, such as were likely to render a judgment on fiction and poetry, or, as the Germans, with better classification, say, in 'DICHTUNG' in general, quite other than the superficial haphazard remarks of which reviews are generally made. You will all the better understand that I have made it a rule not to read writing about myself. I am exceptionally sensitive and liable to discouragement; and to read much remark about my doings would have as depressing an effect on me as staring in a mirror—perhaps, I may say, of defective glass. But my husband looks at all the numerous articles that are forwarded to me, and kindly keeps them out of my way—only on rare occasions reading to me a passage which he thinks will comfort me by its evidence of unusual insight or sympathy. Yesterday he read your article in The Melbourne Review, and said at the end—'This is an excellently written article, which would do credit to any English periodical' adding the very uncommon testimony, 'I shall keep this.' Then he told me of some passages in it which gratified me by that comprehension of my meaning—that laying of the finger on the right spot—which is more precious than praise, and forthwith he went to lay The Melbourne Review in the drawer he assigns to any writing about me that gives him pleasure. For he feels on my behalf more than I feel on my own, at least in matters of this kind. If you come to England again when I happen to be in town I hope that you will give me the pleasure of seeing you under happier auspices than those of your former visit.—I am, dear madam, yours sincerely, M. G. Lewes." The receipt of this kind and candid letter gave me much pleasure; and, although on the strength of that, I cannot boast of being a correspendent of that great woman, I was able to say that I had seen and talked with her, and that she considered me a competent critic of her work. Mrs. Oliphant says that George Eliot's life impelled her to make an involuntary confession—"How have I been handicapped in life? Should I have done better if I had been kept, like her, in a mental green-house and taken care of? I have always had to think of other people and to plan everything for my own pleasure, it is true, very often, but always in subjection to the necessity which bound me to them. To bring up the boys—my own and Frank's—for the service of God was better than to write a fine novel, if it had been in my power to do so." The heart knows its own bitterness. There might have been some points in which George Eliot might have envied Mrs. Oliphant.

CHAPTER X
RETURN FROM THE OLD COUNTRY

Before leaving Scotland I arranged that my friend, Mrs. Graham of the strenuous life and 30 pounds a year, should undertake the care of my aunts, to their mutual satisfaction. My last days in England were spent in either a thick London fog or an equally undesirable Scotch mist, which shrouded everything in obscurity, and made me long for the sunny skies and the clear atmosphere of Australia. I told my friends that in my country it either rained or let it alone. Indeed, the latest news from all Australia was that it had let it alone very badly, and that the overstocking of stations during the preceding good seasons had led to enormous losses. Sheepfarmers made such large profits in good seasons that they were apt to calculate that it was worth while to run the risk of drought; but experience has shown that overstocking does not really pay. The making of dams, the private and public provision of water in the underground reservoirs by artesian bores, and the facilities for travelling stock by such ways have all lessened the risks which the pioneer pastoralists ran bravely in the old days. An Australian drought can never be as disastrous in the twentieth century as it was in 1866; and South Australia, the Central State, has from the first been a pioneer in development as well as in exploration. The hum of the reaping machine first awoke the echoes in our wheatfields. The stump-jumping plough and the mullenicer which beats down the scrub or low bush so that it can be burnt, were South Australian inventions, copied elsewhere, which have turned land accounted worthless into prolific wheat fields.

If South Australia was the first of the States to exhaust her agricultural soil, she was the first to restore it by means of fertilizers and the seed drill. When I see the drilled wheat fields I recollect my grandfather's two silver salvers—the Prizes from the Highland Society for having the largest area of drilled wheat in Scotland—and when I see the grand crops on the Adelaide Plains I recall the opinion that, with anything like a decent rainfall, that soil could grow anything. In 1866 the northern areas had not been opened. The farmers were continuing the process of exhausting the land by growing wheat—wheat—wheat, with the only variety wheaten hay. I recollect James Burnet's amazement when I said that our horses were fed on wheaten hay. "What a waste of the great possibilities of a grain harvest!" He was doubtful when I said that with plenty of wheaten hay the horses needed no corn. South Australia, except about Mount Gambier, does not grow oats, though Victoria depends on oaten hay. The British agriculturist thinks that meadow hay is the natural forage for horses and cattle, and for winter turnips are the standby. It was a little amusing to me that I could speak with some authority to skilled and experienced agriculturists, who felt our rivalry at Mark lane, but who did not dream that with the third great move of Australia towards the markets of the world through cold storage we could send beef, mutton, lamb, poultry, eggs, and all kinds of fruit to the consumers of Europe, and especially of England and its metropolis. I did not see it, any more than the people to whom I talked. I still thought that for meat and all perishable commodities the distance was an insuperable obstacle, and that, except for live stock from America, or canned meat from Australia, the United Kingdom would continue self-supporting on these lines.

I returned to Australia, when this island continent was in the grip of one of the most severe and protracted droughts in its history. The war between Prussia and Austria had begun and ended; the failure of Overend and Gurney and others brought commercial disaster; and my brother, with other bankers, had anxious days and sleepless nights. Some rich men became richer; many poor men went down altogether. Our recovery was slow but sure. In the meantime I found life at home very dull after my interesting experiences abroad. There was nothing to do for proportional representation except to write an occasional letter to the press. So I started another novel, which was published serially in The Observer. Mr. George Bentley, who published it subsequently in book form, changed its title from "Hugh Lindsay's Guest" to "The Author's Daughter." But my development as a public speaker was more important than the publication of a fourth novel. Much had been written on the subject of public speaking by men, but so far nothing concerning the capacities of women in that direction. And yet I think all teachers will agree that girls in the aggregate excel boys in their powers of expression, whether in writing, or in speech, though boys may surpass them in such studies as arithmetic and mathematics. Yet law and custom have put a bridle on the tongue of women, and of the innumerable proverbs relating to the sex, the most cynical are those relating to her use of language. Her only qualification for public speaking in old days was that she could scold, and our ancestors imposed a salutary check on this by the ducking stool in public, and sticks no thicker than the thumb for marital correction in private. The writer of the Proverbs alludes to the perpetual dropping of a woman's tongue as an intolerable nuisance, and declares that it is better to live on the housetop than with a brawling woman in a wide house. A later writer, describing the virtuous woman, said that on her lips is the law of kindness, and after all this is the real feminine characteristic. As daughter, sister, wife, and mother—what does not the world owe to the gracious words, the loving counsel, the ready sympathy which she expresses? Until recent years, however, these feminine Rifts have been strictly kept for home consumption, and only exercised for the woman's family and a limited circle of friends. In 1825, when I first opened my eyes on the world, there were indeed women who displayed an interest in public affairs. My own mother not only felt the keenest solicitude regarding the passing of the Reform Bill, but she took up her pen, and with two letters to the local press, under the signature of "Grizel Plowter," showed the advantages of the proposed measure. But public speaking was absolutely out of the question for women, and though I was the most ambitious of girls, my desire was to write a great book—not at all to sway an audience. When I returned from my first visit to England in 1866, I was asked by the committee of the South Australian Institute to write a lecture on my impressions of England, different from the article which had appeared in The Cornhill Magazine under that title, but neither the committee nor myself thought of the possibility of my delivering it. My good friend, the late Mr. John Howard Clark, Editor of The Register, kindly offered to read it. I did not go to hear it, but I was told that he had difficulty in reading my manuscript, and that, though he was a beautiful reader, it was not very satisfactory. So I mentally resolved that if I was again asked I should offer to read my own MS. Five years afterwards I was asked for two literary lectures by the same committee, and I chose as my subjects the works of Elizabeth Browning and those of her husband, Robert Browning. Now, I consider that the main thing for a lecturer is to be heard, and a rising young lawyer (now our Chief Justice) kindly offered to take the back seat, and promised to raise his hand if he could not hear. It was not raised once, so I felt satisfied. I began by saying that I undertook the work for two reasons—first, to make my audience more familiar with the writings of two poets very dear to me; and second, to make easier henceforward for any woman who felt she had something to say to stand up and say it. I felt very nervous, and as if my knees were giving way; but I did not show any nervousness. I read the lecture, but most of the quotations I recited from memory. Not having had any lessons in elocution, I trusted to my natural voice, and felt that in this new role the less gesticulation I used the better. Whether the advice of Demosthenes is rightly translated or not—first requisite, action; second, action; third, action—I am sure that English word does not express the requisite for women. I should rather call it earnestness—a conviction that what you say is worth saying, and worth saying to the audience before you. I had a lesson on the danger of overaction from hearing a gentleman recite in public "The dream of Eugene Aram," in which he went through all the movements of killing and burying the murdered man. When a tale is crystallized into a poem it does not require the action of a drama. However little action I may use I never speak in public with gloves on. They interfere with the natural eloquence of the hand. After these lectures I occasionally was asked to give others on literary subjects.

At this time I began to study Latin with my nephew, a boy of 14. He was then an orphan, my youngest and beloved sister Mary having recently died and left her two children to my care. My teacher thought me the more apt pupil, but it was really due more to my command of English than to my knowledge of Latin that I was able to get at the meaning of Virgil and Horace. When it came to Latin composition I was no better than the boy of 14.

Before the death of my sister the family invested in land in Trinity street, College Town, and built a house. Mother had planned the house she moved into when I was six months old, and she delighted in the task, though she said it seemed absurd to build a house in her seventy-ninth year. But she lived in it from January, 1870, till December, 1887, and her youngest daughter lived in it for only ten months. Before that time I had embarked with my friend, Miss Clark, on one of the greatest enterprises of my life— one which led to so much that my friends are apt to say that, if I am recollected at all, it will be in connection with the children of the State and not with electoral reform. But I maintain now, as I maintained then, that the main object of my life is proportional representation, or, to use my brother John's term, effective voting.

CHAPTER XI
WARDS OF THE STATE

In a little book which the State Children's Council requested me to write as a memorial of the great work of Miss C. E. Clark on her retirement at the age of 80, I have given an account of the movement from the beginning down to 1907, which had its origin in South Australia under the leadership of Miss Clark. When I was on my way cut from England, Miss Clark wrote a letter to The Register, suggesting that the destitute, neglected, or orphaned children should be removed from the Destitute Asylum and placed in natural homes with respectable people; but the great wave which came over England about that time for building industrial schools and reformatories affected South Australia also, and the idea was that, though the children should be removed from the older inmates, it should be to an institution. Land was bought and plans were drawn up for an industrial school at Magill, five miles from Adelaide, when Miss Clark came to me and asked me to help her to take a different course. She enlisted Mrs. (afterwards Lady) Colton and Mrs. (afterwards Lady) Davenport in the cause, and we arranged for a deputation to the Minister; Howard Clark, Neville Blyth, and Mr. C. B. Young joined us. We offered to find country homes and provide lady visitors, but our request was simply scouted. As we did not offer to bear any of the cost it would be absurd to give us any share in the administration. Children would only be given homes for the sake of the money paid, and Oliver Twist's was held up as the sort of apprenticeship likely to be secured for pauper children. So we had to play the waiting game. The school built to accommodate 230 children was on four floors, though there was 40 acres of good land. It was so popular that, though only 130 went in at first, in two years it was so full that there was talk of adding a wing. This was our opportunity, and the same men and women went on another deputation, and this time we prevailed, and were allowed to place out the overflow as an experiment; and not only the Boarding-out Committee, but the official heads of the

Destitute Department, were surprised and delighted with the good homes we secured for 5/ a week, and with the improvement in health, in intelligence, and in happiness that resulted from putting children into natural homes. What distinguishes work for children in Australia from what is done elsewhere is that it is national, and not philanthropic. The State is in loco-parentis, and sees that what the child needs are a home and a mother—that, if the home and the mother are good, the child shall be kept there; but that vigilant inspection is needed, voluntary or official—better to have both. Gradually the Magill School was emptied, and the children were scattered. Up to the age of 13 the home was subsidized, but when by the education law the child was free from school attendance, and went to service, the supervision continued until the age of 18 was reached. For nearly 14 years, from 1872 to 1886, the Boarding-out Society pursued its modest labours as auxiliary to the Destitute Board. Our volunteer visitors reported in duplicate—one copy for the official board, and one for the unofficial committee. When the method was inaugurated, Mr. T. S. Reed. Chairman of the Board, was completely won over. We had nothing to do with the reformatories, except that our visitors went to see those placed out at service in their neighbourhood.

Our success attracted attention elsewhere. The late Dr. Andrew Garran, who was on The Register when I went to England, had moved to Sydney in my absence, and was on the staff of The Sydney Morning Herald. When Miss Clark went to England in 1877, after her mother's death, Dr. Garran wrote to me for some account of our methods, and of their success, physical, moral, and financial. Dr. Garran came out with Mr. G. F. Angas and the Australian Constitution in 1851 in search of health and work, both of which he found here. The first pages of my four volumes of newspaper cuttings are filled with two long articles, "The Children of the State," and this started the movement in New South Wales, led by Mrs. Garran, nee Sabine, and Mrs. Jefferis wife of the leading Congregational minister, moved from Adelaide to Sydney. Professor Henry Pearson asked me a year or two later to give similar information to The Melbourne Age. Subsequently I wrote on this subject, by request, to Queensland, New Zealand, and I think also Tasmania, where we were imitated first, but where there are still to be found children of the State in institutions. In Victoria and New South Wales a vigorous policy emptied these buildings, which were used for other public purposes, and the children were dispersed. The innovation which at first was scouted as utopian, next suspected as leading to neglect, or even unkindness—for people would only take these children for what they could make out of them—was found to be so beneficial that nobody in Australia would like to return to the barrack home or the barrack school. If the inspection had been from the first merely official, public opinion would have been suspicious and sceptical, but when ladies saw the children in these homes, and watched how the dull faces brightened, and the languid limbs became alert after a few weeks of ordinary life—when the cheeks became rosier, and the eyes had new light in them; when they saw that the foster parents took pride in their progress at school, and made them handy about the house, as they could never be at an institution, where everything is done at the sound of a bell or the stroke of a clock—these ladies testified to what they knew, and the public believed in them. In other English-speaking countries boarding-out in families is sometimes permitted; but here, under the Southern Cross, it is the law of the land that children shall not be brought up in institutions, but in homes: that the child whose parent is the State shall have as good schooling as the child who has parents and guardians; that every child shall have, not the discipline of routine and redtape, but free and cheerful environment of ordinary life, preferably in the country—going to school with other young fellow citizens, going to church with the family in which he is placed, having the ordinary ditties, the ordinary difficulties, the ordinary pleasures of common life; but guarded from injustice, neglect, and cruelty by effective and kindly supervision. This movement, originated in South Australia, and with all its far-reaching developments and expansions, is due to the initiative of one woman of whom the State is justly proud—Miss Caroline Emily Clark.

Even while we were only a Boarding-out Committee, it was found necessary to have one paid inspector; but there was great dissatisfaction with the Boys' Reformatory which had been located in an old leaky hulk, where the boys could learn neither seamanship nor anything else—and with some other details of the management of the destitute poor, and a commission with the Chief Justice as Chairman, was appointed to make enquiries and suggest reforms. The result was the separation of the young from the old absolutely; and a new body, the State Children's Council, of 12 men and women of nearly equal proportions, had authority over the reformatories, as well as what was called the industrial school, which was to be reduced to a mere receiving home, and all the children placed out, either on subsidy or at service. Most of the old committee were appointed; but, to my great joy, Dr. Edward C. Stirling and Mr. James Smith, the most enlightened man on the Destitute Board, were among the new members. We had a paid stall, with a most able secretary—Mr. J. B. Whiting.

Dr. Stirling was unanimously voted in as President, and we felt we began our new duties under the most promising auspices. But, alas, in two years there was so much friction between the council and the Ministry that we all resigned in a body, except Mrs. Colton (who was in England) and Mrs. Farr. We were fighting the battle of the unpaid boards, and we were so strong in the public estimation that we might have won the victory. The Government had relieved children on the petition of parents, contrary to the strong recommendation of the council. Although the commission had declared that the reformatory boys should be removed at once from the hulk Fitzjames, they were still kept there, and the only offer of accommodation given was to share the Magill Industrial School with the reformatory girls. Now, this the council would not hear of, for we felt that the Government plans for separate entrances and separate staircases were absolutely futile and ridiculous for keeping apart these two dangerous classes in a single building. The Government gave way on the point of providing a separate building for the reformatory girls; and the committee, with the exception of Dr. Stirling and Mr. James Smith—our two strongest members—were reappointed. The official staff was increased by the appointment of clerks and inspectors, many of them women, who have always given every satisfaction, and who justify the claim made that women's work is conscientious and thorough.

More departments were gradually added to our sphere of action. The separate trial of juvenile delinquents was strongly advocated by the council. Miss Clark and Mr. C. H. Goode were particularly keen on the introduction of Children's Courts. In this reform South Australia led the world, and in the new Act of 1896, after six years of tentative work, it became compulsory to try offenders under 18 at the Children's Court in the city and suburbs, and in the Magistrate's room in the country. The methods of organization and control vary in the different States of the Commonwealth, but on one point the six are all agreed—that dependent and delinquent children are a national asset and a national responsibility, and any forward step anywhere has every chance of being copied. The result of Children's Courts and probation has been that, while the population of the State has greatly increased, the committals to the Gaol and for penal servitude have steadily decreased, and the Boys' Reformatory has been reduced to one-third of the number in earlier days. There are, of course, many factors in all directions of social betterment, but the substitution of homes for institutions, and of probation carefully watched for summary punishment, are, in my opinion, the largest factors in, this State. The affection between children and their foster parents is often lifelong; and we see thousands who were taken from bad parents and evil environments taking their place in the industrial world, and filling it well. The movement in South Australia initiated by Miss Clark spread from State to State, and the happy thought of the President and Secretary of the Council that I should write an account of "Boarding-out and its Developments" as a memorial of her great work bore fruit in the legislation of the United Kingdom itself. A letter I received from Mr. Herbert Samuel, then Under-Secretary of State in the British Government, was gratifying, both to the council and to me:—"Home Office, Whitehall, S.W., August 5, 1907. Dear Madam—I have just read your little book on 'State Children in Australia;' and, although a stranger to you, would venture to write to thank you for the very valuable contribution you have made to the literature on the subject. The present Government in England are already engaged in promoting the more kindly and more effective methods of dealing with destitute, neglected, or delinquent children, which are already so widely adopted in South Australia. We are passing through Parliament this year a Bill to enable a system of probation officers, both paid and voluntary, to be established throughout the country, for dealing not indeed with child offenders alone, but with adult offenders also, who may be properly amenable to that treatment. And next year we propose to introduce a comprehensive Children's Bill, which has been entrusted to my charge, in which we hope to be able to include some of the reforms you have at heart. In the preparation of that Bill the experience of your colony and the account of it which you have published will be of no small assistance. Yours sincerely, Herbert Samuel."

Another department of our work for the protection of infant life, and this we took over from the Destitute Board, where some unique provisions had been initiated by Mr. James Smith. The Destitute Asylum was the last refuge of the old and incapacitated poor, but it never opened its doors to the able bodied. In the Union Workhouse in England room is always found for friendless and penniless to come there for confinement, who leave as soon as they are physically strong enough to take their burden—their little baby—in their arms and face the world again. In Adelaide these women were in 1868 divided into two classes, one for girls who had made their first slip—girls weak, but very rarely wicked—so as to separate them, from women who came for a second or third time, who were cared for with their infants in the general asylum. Mr. James Smith obtained in 1881 legislation to empower the Destitute Board to make every woman sign an agreement to remain with her infant, giving it the natural nourishment, for six months. This has saved many infant lives, and has encouraged maternal affection. The Destitute Board kept in its hands the issuing of licences, and appointed a lady to visit the babies till they were two years old, and did good work; but when that department was properly turned over to the State Children's Council there was even more vigilance exercised, and the death rate among these babies, often handicapped before birth, and always artificially fed after, was reduced to something less than the average of all babies. We have been fortunate in our chief inspectress of babies. Her character has uplifted the licensed foster mothers, and the two combined have raised the real mothers. It is surprising how few such babies are thrown on the State. The department does not pay any board or find any clothing for these infants. It, however, pays for supervision and pays for a lady doctor, so that there need be no excuse for not calling in medical assistance if it is felt to be needed. Occasionally a visitor from other States or from England is allowed as a great favour to see, not picked cases, but the ordinary run, of the homes of foster mothers, and the question, "Where and how do you get such women?" is asked. We have weeded out the inferiors, and our instructions with regard to feeding and care are so definite, and found to be so sound, that the women take a pride in the health and the beauty of the little ones; and besides they keep up the love of the real mother by the care they give them. A recent Act has raised the age of supervision of illegitimate babies from two to seven years, and this has necessitated the appointment of an additional inspectress. In South Australia baby farming has been extinguished, and in the other States legislation on similar lines has been won, and they are in process of gradually weeding out bad and doubtful foster mothers. And the foster fathers are often as fond of the babies as their wives—and as softhearted. "Did you see that the poor girl had on broken boots this weather?" said he. "Yes, it's a Pity; but we are poor folks ourselves—we can't help it," said she. "Let her off the 6/ for a fortnight, so as she can get a pair of sound boots for her feet, we'll worry through without it." And they did. The extreme solicitude of the State Children's Department, as carried out by its zealous officers, for the life and the wellbeing of their babies serves them in Public extenuation, and the children are often so pretty and engaging that they win love all round. A grown-up son in the home was very fond of little Lily. "Mother will you get Lily a cream coat, such as I see other babies wearing, and I will pay for it."

A most pathetic story I can tell of a girl respectably connected in the country, who had been cast off in disgrace, and came to town to take a place, committing her infant to a good foster mother. When he was old enough to move about, and was just trying to walk, the mother was taken dangerously ill to the Adelaide Hospital. The foster mother thought the girl's father should be sent for, and wrote to him giving her own address, but not disclosing her connection with the patient. The father of the girl came, and was told that he had better be accompanied by his informant, who could prepare the sick woman for the interview. The little boy was running about, and the old man took him on his knee while the woman got ready to go out. "You must come with us, Sonny," said she. "I can't leave you alone in the house." "A very fine little chap. Your youngest, I suppose. I can see he is a great pet." "No," said the woman slowly, "he is not my son, he is your grandson." "Good God, my grandson," Then, clasping the little fellow to his heart, he said, "I'll never part with him!" The mother recovered, and was taken home with her child and forgiven. Such is often the work of the good foster mother. In all the successes of the irresponsible committee and of the responsible State Children's Council the greatest factor has been the character of the good women who have been mothers to the little ones. The fears that only self-interest could induce them to take on the neglected and uncontrollable children were not borne out by experience, and in the ease of these babies not really illegitimate—it is the parents who deserve that title, no infant can—the mother's instinct came out very strong. At a conference of workers among dependent children, held in Adelaide in May, 1909, when all six States were represented, a Western Australian representative said that the average family home was not so good for its natural circle that it could be depended on for strangers; but our answer was that, both for the children of the State and for the babies who were not State children, we insisted on something better than the average home, and through our inspection we sought to improve it still further. We have not reached perfection by any means. When we begin to think we have, we are sure to fall back. Another good office the State Children's Department fills is that of advice gratis. One of the most striking chapters in Gen. Booth's "Darkest England" dealt with the helplessness of the poor and the ignorant in the face of difficulties, of injustice, and of extortion. When I was in Chicago in 1893 I saw that the first university settlement, that of Hull House, presided over by Miss Jane Addams (St. Jane some of her friends call her) was the centre to is which the poor American, German, Italian, or other alien went for advice as well as practical help. A word in season was often of more value than dollars. To be told what to do or what not to do at a crisis when decision is so important may be salvation for the pocket or for the character.

CHAPTER XII
PREACHING, FRIENDS, AND WRITING

My life now became more interesting and varied. A wider field for my journalistic capabilities was open to me, and I also took part in the growth of education, both spiritual and secular. The main promoters of the ambitious literary periodical The Melbourne Review, to which I became a contributor, were Mr. Henry Gyles Turner (the banker), Mr. Alexander Sutherland, M.A. (author of "The History of Australia" and several other books), and A. Patchett Martin (the litterateur). It lived for nine years, and produced a good deal of creditable writing, but it never was able to pay its contributors, because it never attained such a circulation as would attract advertisements. The reviews and magazines of the present day depend on advertisements. They cheapen the price so as to gain a circulation, which advertisers cater for. I think my second article was on the death of Sir Richard Hanson (one of the original South Australian Literary Society, which met in London before South Australia existed). At the time of his death he was Chief Justice. He was the author of two books of Biblical criticism—"The Jesus of History" and "Paul and the Primitive Church"—and I undertook to deal with his life and work. About that time there was one of those periodic outbursts of Imperialism in the Australian colonies—not popular or general, but among politicians—on the question of how the colonies could obtain practical recognition in the Legislature of the United Kingdom. Each of the colonies felt that Downing street inadequately represented its claims and its aspirations, and there were several articles in "The Melbourne Review" suggesting that these colonies should be allowed to send members to the House of Commons. This, I felt, would be inadmissible; for, unless we were prepared to bear our share of the burdens, we had no right to sit in the taxing Assembly of the United Kingdom. The only House in which the colonies, small or great, could be represented was the House of Lords; and it appeared to me that, with a reformed House of Lords, this would be quite practicable. An article in

Fraser's Magazine, "Why not the Lords, too?" had struck me much, and the lines on which it ran greatly resemble those laid down by Lord Rosebery for lessening in number and improving in character the unwieldy hereditary House of Peers; but neither that writer nor Lord Rosebery grasped the idea that I made prominent in an article I wrote for The Review, which was that the reduction of the peers to 200, or any other number ought to be made on the principle of proportional representation, because otherwise the majority of the peers, being Conservative, an election on ordinary lines would result in a selection of the most extreme Conservatives in the body. My mother had pointed out to me that the 16 representative Scottish peers elected by those who have not a seat as British peers, for the duration of each Parliament, were the most Tory of the Tories, and that the same could be said of the 28 representative peers for Ireland elected for life. So, though the House of Lords contains a respectable minority of Liberals, under no system of exclusively majority representation could any of them be chosen among the 200. I had the same idea of life peers to be added from the ranks of the professions, of science, and of literature, unburdened by the weight and cost of an hereditary title, that Lord Rosebery has; and into such a body I thought that representatives of the great self-governing colonies could enter, so that information about our resources, our politics, and our sociology might be available, and might permeate the press. But, greatly to my surprise, my article was sent back, but was afterwards accepted by Fraser's Magazine. This was better for me, for what would have been published for nothing in The Melbourne Review brought me 8/15/0 from a good English magazine. I continued to write for this review, until it ceased to exist, in 1885, literary and political articles. The former included a second one on "George Eliot's Life and Work," and one on "Honore de Balzac," which many of my friends thought my best literary effort.

It was through Miss Martha Turner that I was introduced to her brother and to The Melbourne Review. She was at that time pastor of the Unitarian Church in Melbourne. She had during the long illness of the Rev. Mr. Higginson helped her brother with the services. At first she wrote sermons for him to deliver, but on some occasions when he was indisposed she read her own compositions. Fine reader as Mr. H. G. Turner is he did not come up to her, and especially he could not equal her in the presentment of her own thoughts. The congregation on the death of Mr. Higginson asked Miss Turner to accept the pastorate. She said she could conduct the services, but she absolutely declined to do the pastoral duties—visiting especially. She was licensed to conduct marriage services and baptized (or, as we call it, consecrated) children to the service of Almighty God and to the service of man. During the absence of our pastor for a long holiday in England Mr. C. L. Whitham afterwards an education inspector, took his place for two years, and he arranged for an exchange of three weeks with Miss Turner. She is the first woman I ever heard in the pulpit. I was thrilled by her exquisite voice, by her earnestness, and by her reverence. I felt as I had never felt before that if women are excluded from the Christian pulpit you shut out more than half of the devoutness that is in the world. Reading George Eliot's description of Dinah Morris preaching Methodisim on the green at Hayslope had prepared me in a measure, but when I heard a highly educated and exceptionally able woman conducting the services all through, and especially reading the Scriptures of the Old and New Testaments with so much intelligence that they seemed to take on new meaning, I felt how much the world had been losing for so many centuries. She twice exchanged with Adelaide—the second time when Mr. Woods had returned—and it was the beginning to me of a close friendship.

Imitation, they say, is the sincerest flattery; and when a similar opportunity was offered to me during an illness of Mr. Woods, when no layman was available, I was first asked to read a sermon of Martineau's and then I suggested that I might give something of my own. My first original sermon was on "Enoch and Columbus," and my second on "Content, discontent, and uncontent." I suppose I have preached more than a hundred times, in my life, mostly in the Wakefield Street pulpit; but in Melbourne and Sydney I am always asked for help; and when I went to America in 1893-4 I was offered seven pulpits—one in Toronto, Canada, and six in the United States. The preparation of my sermons—for, after the first one I delivered, they were always original—has always been a joy and delight to me, for I prefer that my subjects as well as their treatment shall be as humanly helpful as it is possible to make them. In Sydney particularly I have preached to fine audiences. On one occasion I remember preaching in a large hall, as the Unitarian Church could not have held the congregation. It was during the campaign that Mrs. Young and I conducted in Sydney—in 1900, and we had spent the day—a delightful one—with the present Sir George and Lady Reid at their beautiful home at Strathfield, and returned in time to take the evening service at Sydney. I spoke on the advantages of international peace, and illustrated my discourse with arguments, drawn from the South African War, which was then in progress. I seized the opportunity afforded me of speaking some plain home truths on the matter. I was afterwards referred to by The Sydney Bulletin as "the gallant little old lady who had more moral courage in her little finger than all the Sydney ministers had in their combined anatomies." For one of my sermons I wrote an original parable which pleased my friends so much that I include it in the account of my life's work. "And it came to pass after the five days of Creation which were periods of unknown length of time that God took the soul, the naked soul, with which He was to endow the highest of his creatures—into Eden to look with him on the work which He had accomplished. And the Soul could see, could hear, could understand, though there were neither eyes, nor ears, nor limbs, nor bodily organs, to do its bidding. And God said, 'Soul, thou shalt have a body as these creatures, that thou seest around thee have. Thou art to be king, and rule over them all. Thy mission is to subdue the earth, and make it fruitful and more beautiful than it is even now, in thus its dawn. Which of all these living creatures wouldst thou resemble?' And the Soul looked, and the Soul listened, and the Soul understood. The beauty of the birds first attracted him and their songs were sweet, and their loving care of their young called forth a response in the Prophetic Soul. But the sweet singers could not subdue the earth—nay, even the strongest voice could not. Then the Soul gazed on the lion in his strength; on the deer in his beauty. He saw the large-eyed bull with the cow by his side, licking her calf. The stately horse, the huge elephant, the ungainly camel—could any of these subdue the earth? He looked down, and they made it shake with their heavy tread, but the Soul knew that the earth could not be subdued by them. Then he saw a pair of monkeys climbing a tree—the female had a little one in her arms. Where the bird had wings, and the beasts four legs planted on the ground, the monkeys had arms, and, at the end of each, hands, with five fingers; they gathered nuts and cracked them, and picked out the kernels, throwing the shells away—the mother caressed her young one with gentle fingers. The Soul saw also the larger ape with its almost upright form. 'Ah!' sighed the Soul, 'they are not beautiful like the other creatures, neither are they so strong as many of them. But their forelimbs, with hands and fingers to grasp with, are what I need to subdue the earth, for they will be the servants who can best obey my will. Let me stand upright and gaze upward, and this is the body that I choose.' And God said, 'Soul, thou hast chosen well, Thou shalt be larger and stronger than these creatures thou seest thou shalt stand upright, and look upward and onward. And the Soul can create beauty for itself, when it shines through the body.' And it was so, and Adam stood erect and gave names to all other creatures."

In the seventies the old education system, or want of system, was broken up, and a complete department of public instruction was constructed. Mr. J. A. Hartley, head master of Prince Alfred College, was placed at the head of it, and a vigorous policy was adopted. When the Misses Davenport Hill came out to visit aunt and cousins, I visited with them and Miss Clark the Grote Street Model School, and I was delighted with the new administration. I hoped that the instruction of the children of the people would attract the poor gentlewomen who were so badly paid as governesses in families or in schools; but my hope has not been at all adequately fulfilled. The Register had been most earnest in its desire for a better system of public education. The late Mr. John Howard Clark, its then editor, wanted some articles on the education of girls, and he applied to me to do them, and I wrote two leading articles on the subject, and another on the "Ladder of Learning." from the elementary school to the university, as exemplified in my native country where ambitious lads cultivated literature on a little oatmeal. For an Adelaide University was in the air, and took form owing to the benefactions of Capt. (afterwards Sir Walter Watson) Hughes, and Mr. (afterwards Sir Thomas) Elder. But the opposition to Mr. Hartley, which set in soon after his appointment, and his supposed drastic methods and autocratic attitude, continued. I did not knew Mr. Hartley personally, but I knew he had been an admirable head teacher, and the most valuable member of the Education Board which preceded the revolution. I knew, too, that the old school teachers were far inferior to what were needed for the new work, and that you cannot make an omelette without breaking eggs. A letter which I wrote to Mr. Hartley, saying that I desired to help him in any way in my power, led to a friendship which lasted till his lamented death in 1896. I fancied at the time that my aid did him good, but I think now that the opposition had spent its force before I put in my oar by some letters to the press. South Australians became afterwards appreciative of the work done by Mr. Hartley, and proud of the good position this State took in matters educational among the sister States under the Southern Cross.

It was due to Mrs. Webster's second visit to Adelaide to exchange with Mr. Woods that I made the acquaintance of Mr. and Mrs. E. Barr Smith. They went to the church and were shown into my seat, and Mrs. Smith asked me to bring the eloquent preacher to Torrens Park to dine there. I discovered that they had long wanted to know me, but I was out of society. I recollect afterwards going to the office to see Mr. Smith on some business or other, when he was out, and meeting Mr. Elder instead. He pressed on me the duty of going to see Mrs. Black, a lady from Edinburgh, who had come out with her sons and daughter. Mr. Barr Smith came in, and his brother-in-law said, "I have just been telling Miss Spence she should go and call on the Blacks." "Tom," said Mr. Barr Smith, "we have been just 20 years making the acquaintance of Miss Spence. About the year 1899 Miss Spence will be dropping in on the Blacks." What a house Torrens Park was for books. There was no other customer of the book shops equal to the Torrens Park family. Rich men and women often buy books for themselves, and for rare old books they will give big prices; but the Barr Smiths bought books in sixes and in dozens for the joy of giving them where they would be appreciated. On my literary side Mrs. Barr Smith, a keen critic herself, fitted in with me admirably, and what I owed to her in the way of books for about 10 years cannot be put on paper, and in my journalistic work she delighted. Other friendships, both literary and personal, were formed in the decade which started the elementary schools and the University. The first Hughes professor of English literature was the Rev. John Davidson of Chalmers Church, married to Harriet, daughter of Hugh Miller, the self-taught ecologist and journalist.

On the day of the inauguration of the University the Davidsons asked Miss Clark and myself to go with them, and there I met Miss Catherine Mackay (now Mrs. Fred Martin), from Mount Gambier. I at first thought her the daughter of a wealthy squatter of the south-east, but when I found she was a litterateur trying to make a living by her pen, bringing out a serial tale, "Bohemian Born," and writing occasional articles, I drew to her at once. So long as the serial tale lasted she could hold her own; but no one can make a living at occasional articles in Australia, and she became a clerk in the Education Office, but still cultivated literature in her leisure hours. She has published two novels—"An Australian Girl" and "The Silent Sea"—which so good a judge as F. W. H. Myers pronounced to be on the highest level ever reached in Australian fiction, and in that opinion I heartily concur. I take a very humble second place beside her, but in the seventies I wrote "Gathered In," which I believed to be my best novel—the novel into which I put the most of myself, the only novel I wrote with tears of emotion. Mrs. Oliphant says that Jeanie Deans is more real to her than any of her own creations, and probably it is the same with me, except for this one work. From an old diary of the fifties, when my first novels were written I take this extract:— "Queer that I who have such a distinct idea of what I approve in flesh-and-blood men should only achieve in pen and ink a set of impossible people, with an absurd muddy expression of gloom, instead of sublime depth as I intended. Men novelists' women are as impossible creations as my men, but there is this difference— their productions satisfy them, mine fail to satisfy me." But in my last novel—still unpublished—felt quite satisfied that I had at last achieved my ambition to create characters that stood out distinctly and real. Miss Clark took the MS. to England, but she could not get either Bentley or Smith Elder, or Macmillan to accept it.

On the death of Mr. John Howard Clark, which took place at this time, Mr. John Harvey Finlayson was left to edit The Register, and I became a regular outside contributor to The Register and The Observer. He desired to keep up and if possible improve the literary side of the papers, and felt that the loss of Mr. Clark might be in some measure made up if I give myself wholeheartedly to the work. Leading articles were to be written at my own risk. If they suited the policy of the paper they would be accepted, otherwise not. What a glorious opening for my ambition and for my literary proclivities came to me in July, 1878, when I was in my fifty-third year! Many leading articles were rejected, but not one literary or social article. Generally these last appeared in both daily and weekly papers. I recollect the second original social article I wrote was on "Equality as an influence on society and manners," suggested by Matthew Arnold. The much-travelled Smythe, then, I think, touring with Charles Clark, wrote to Mr. Finlayson from Wallaroo thus:—"In this dead-alive place, where one might fire a mitrailleuse down the principal street without hurting anybody, I read this delightful article in yesterday's Register. When we come again to Adelaide, and we collect a few choice spirits, be sure to invite the writer of this article to join us." I felt as if the round woman had got at last into the round hole which fitted her; and in my little study, with my books and my pigeon holes, and my dear old mother sitting with her knitting on her rocking chair at the low window, I had the knowledge that she was interested in all I did. I generally read the MS to her before it went to the office. What is more remarkable, perhaps, is that the excellent maid who was with us for 12 years, picked out everything of mine that was in the papers and read it. A series of papers called "Some Social Aspects of Early Colonial Life" I contributed under the pseudonym of "A Colonist of 1839." From 1878 till 1893, when I went round the world via America, I held the position of outside contributor on the oldest newspaper in the State, and for these 14 years I had great latitude. My friend Dr. Garran, then editor of The Sydney Morning Herald, accepted reviews and articles from me. Sometimes I reviewed the same books for both, but I wrote the articles differently, and made different quotations, so that I scarcely think any one could detect the same hand in them; but generally they were different books and different subjects, which I treated. I tried The Australasian with a short story, "Afloat and Ashore," and with a social article on "Wealth, Waste, and Want." I contributed to The Melbourne Review, and later to The Victorian Review, which began by paying well, but filtered out gradually. I found journalism a better paying business for me than novel writing, and I delighted in the breadth of the canvas on which I could draw my sketches of books and of life. I believe that my work on newspapers and reviews is more characteristic of me, and intrinsically better work than what I have done in fiction; but when I began to wield the pen, the novel was the line of least resistance. When I was introduced in 1894 to Mrs. Croly, the oldest woman journalist in the United States, as an Australian journalist, I found that her work, though good enough, was essentially woman's work, dress, fashions, functions, with educational and social outlooks from the feminine point of view. My work might show the bias of sex, but it dealt with the larger questions which were common to humanity; and when I recall the causes which I furthered, and which in some instances I started, I feel inclined to magnify the office of the anonymous contributor to the daily press. And I acknowledge not only the kindness of friends who put some of the best new books in my way, but the large-minded tolerance of the Editors of The Register, who gave me such a free hand in the treatment of books, of men, and of public questions.

CHAPTER XIII
MY WORK FOR EDUCATION

I was the first woman appointed on a Board of Advice under the Education Department, and found the work interesting. The powers of the board were limited to an expenditure of 5 pounds for repairs without applying to the department and to interviewing the parents of children who had failed to attend the prescribed number of days, as well as those who pleaded poverty as an excuse for the non-payment of fees. I always felt that the school fees were a heavy burden on the poor, and rejoiced accordingly when free education was introduced into South Australia. This was the second State to adopt this great reform, Victoria preceding it by a few years. I objected to the payment of fees on another ground. I felt they bore heavily on the innocent children themselves through the notion of caste which was created in the minds of those who paid fees to the detriment of their less fortunate school companions. And again, education that is compulsory should be free. Other women have since become members of School Boards, but I was the pioneer of that branch of public work for women in this State. It is a privilege that American women have been fighting for for many years—to vote for and to be eligible to sit on School Boards. In many of the States this has been won to their great advantage. In this present year of 1910 Mrs. Ella, Flagg Young, at the age of 65, has been elected by the Chigago Board, Director of the Education of that great city of over two millions of inhabitants at a salary of 2,000 pounds a year, with a male university professor as an assistant. At an age when we in South Australia are commanding our teachers to retire, in Chicago, which is said by Foster Fraser to cashier men at 40, this elderly woman has entered into her great power.

It is characteristic of me that I like to do thoroughly what I undertake to do at all, and when, on one occasion I had not received the usual summons to attend a board meeting, I complained of the omission to the Chairman. "I do not want," I said, "to be a merely ornamental member of this board. I want to go to all the meetings." He replied, courteously, "It is the last thing that we would say of you, Miss Spence, that you are ornamental!" It was half a minute before he discovered that he had put his disclaimer in rather a different form from what he had intended, and he joined in the burst of laughter which followed. Another amusing contretemps occurred when the same gentleman and I were visiting the parents who had pleaded for exemption from the payment of fees. At one house there was a grown-up daughter who had that morning left the service of the gentleman's mother— a fact enlarged upon by my companion during the morning's drive. "Why is your eldest daughter out of a place?" was the first question he put to the woman. "She might be earning good wages, and be able to help you pay the fees." "Oh!" came the unexpected reply, "she had to leave old Mrs. —— this morning; she was that mean there was no living in the house with her!" Knowing her interlocutor only as the man in authority, the unfortunate woman scarcely advanced her cause by her plain speaking, and I was probably the only member of the trio who appreciated the situation. I am sure many people who were poorer than this mother paid the fees rather than suffer the indignity of such cross-questioning by the school visitors and the board—an unfortunate necessity of the system, which disappeared with the abolition of school fees.

It had been suggested by the Minister of Education of that period that the children attending the State schools should be instructed in the duties of citizenship, and that they should be taught something of the laws under which they lived, and I was commissioned to write a short and pithy statement of the case. It was to be simple enough for intelligent children in the fourth class; 11 or 12—it was to lead from the known to the unknown— it might include the elements of political economy and sociology—it might make use of familiar illustrations from the experience of a new country—but it must not be long. It was not very easy to satisfy myself and Mr. Hartley—who was a severe critic—but when the book of 120 pages was completed he was satisfied. A preface I wrote for the second edition—the first 5,000 copies being insufficient for the requirements of the schools—will give some idea of the plan of the work:—"In writing this little book, I have aimed less at symmetrical perfection than at simplicity of diction, and such arrangement as would lead from the known to the unknown, by which the older children in our public schools might learn not only the actual facts about the laws they live under, but also some of the principles which underlie all law." The reprinting gave me an opportunity to reply to my critics that "political economy, trades unions, insurance companies, and newspapers" were outside the scope of the laws we live under. But I thought that in a new State where the optional duties of the Government are so numerous, it was of great importance for the young citizen to understand economic principles. As conduct is the greater part of life, and morality, not only the bond of social union, but the main source of individual happiness, I took the ethical part of the subject first, and tried to explain that education was of no value unless it was used for good purposes. As without some wealth, civilization was impossible, I next sought to show that national and individual wealth depends on the security that is given by law, and on the industry and the thrift which that security encourages. Land tenure is of the first importance in colonial prosperity, and consideration of the land revenue and the limitations as to its expenditure led me to the necessity for taxation and the various modes of levying it. Taxation led me to the power which imposes, collects, and expends it. This involved a consideration of those representative institutions which make the Government at once the master and the servant of the people. Under this Government our persons and our prosperity are protected by a system of criminal, civil, and insolvent law—each considered in its place. Although not absolutely included in the laws we live under, I considered that providence, and its various outlets in banks, savings banks, joint stock companies, friendly societies, and trades unions, were matters too important to be left unnoticed; and also those influences which shape character quite as much as statute laws—public opinion, the newspaper, and amusements. As the use of my little book was restricted solely to school hours, my hope that the parents might be helped and encouraged by its teaching was doomed to disappointment. But the children of 30 years ago, when "The Laws We Live Under" was first published, are the men and women of to-day, and who shall say but that among them are to be found some at least worthy and true citizens, who owe to my little book their first inspiration to "hitch their wagon to a star." Last year an enthusiastic young Swedish teacher and journalist was so taken with this South Australian little handbook of civics that he urged on me the duty of bringing it up to date, and embracing women's suffrage, the relations of the States to the Commonwealth, as well as the industrial legislation which is in many ways peculiar to Australia, but although those in authority were sympathetic no steps have been taken for its reproduction. Identified as I had been for so many years with elementary education in South Australia, my mind was well prepared to applaud the movement in favour of the higher education of poorer children of both sexes by the foundation of bursaries and scholarships, and the opening up of the avenues of learning to women by admitting them to University degrees. Victoria was the first to take this step, and all over the Commonwealth the example has been followed. I am, however, somewhat disappointed that University women are not more generally progressive in their ideas. They have won something which I should have been very glad of, but which was quite out of reach. All opportunities ought to be considered as opportunities for service. As my brother David regarded the possession of honours and wealth as demanding sacrifice for the common good, so I regarded special knowledge and special culture as means for advancing the culture of all. It is said to be human nature when special privileges or special gifts are used only for egoistic ends; but the complete development of the human being demands that altruistic ideas should also be cultivated. We see that in China an aristocracy of letters—for it is through passing difficult examinations in old literature that the ruling classes are appointed—is no protection to the poor and ignorant from oppression or degradation. It is true that the classics in China are very old, but so are the literatures of Greece and Rome, on which so many university degrees are founded; and it ought to be impressed upon all seekers after academic honours that personal advantage is not the be-all and end-all of their pursuits. In our democratic Commonwealth, although there are some lower titles bestowed by the Sovereign on colonists more or less distinguished, these are not hereditary, so that an aristocracy is not hereditary. There may be an upper class, based on landed estate or one on business success, or one on learning, but all tend to become conservative as conservatism is understood in Australia. Safety is maintained by the free rise from the lower to the higher. But all the openings to higher education offered in high school and university do not tempt the working man's children who want to earn wages as soon as the law lets them go to work. Nor do they tempt their parents to their large share of the sacrifice which young Scotch lads and even American lads make to get through advanced studies. The higher education is still a sort of preserve of the well-to-do, and when one thinks of how greatly this is valued it seems a pity that it is not open to the talents, to the industry, to the enthusiasm of all the young of both sexes. But one exception I must make to the aloofness of people with degrees and professions from the preventible evils of the world, and that is in the profession that is the longest and the most exacting—the medical profession. The women doctors whom I have met in Adelaide, Melbourne, and Sydney have a keen sense of their responsibility to the less fortunate. That probably is because medicine as now understood and practised is the most modern of the learned professions, and is more human than engineering, which is also modern. It takes us into the homes of the poor more intimately than even the clergyman, and it offers remedies and palliatives as well as advice. The law is little studied by women in Australia, but in the United States there are probably a thousand or more legal practitioners. It is the profession that I should have chosen when I was young if it had been in any way feasible. I had no bent for the medical profession, and still less for what every one thinks the most womanly of avocations—that of the trained nurse. I could nurse my own relatives more or less well, but did not distinguish myself in that way, and I could not devote myself to strangers. The manner in which penniless young men become lawyers in the United States seems impossible in Australia. Judge Lindsay, son of a ruined southern family, studied law and delivered newspapers in the morning, worked in a lawyer's office through the day, and acted as janitor at night. The course appears to be shorter, and probably less Latin and Greek were required in a western State than here. But during the long vacation in summer, students go as waiters in big hotels at seaside or other health resorts, or take up some other seasonal trade. All the Columbian guards at the Chicago Exhibition were students. They kept order, they gave directions, they wheeled invalids in bath chairs, and they earned all that was needed, for their next winter's course. In the long high school holidays youths and maidens who are poor and ambitious work for money. I have seen fairly well-paid professors who went back to the father's farm and worked hard all harvest time—and students always did so. It appears easier in America to get a job for three months' vacation than in England or Australia, and the most surprising thing about an American is his versatility. Teaching is with most American men only a step to something better, so that almost all elementary and the far greater proportion of high school teaching is in the hands of women. In Australia our male teachers have to spend so many years before they are fully equipped that they rarely leave the profession. The only check on the supply is that the course is so long and laborious that the youth prefers an easy clerkship. Women, in spite of the chance of marriage, enter the profession in the United States in greater numbers, and as the scale of salaries is by no means equal pay for equal work, except in New York, money is saved by employing women. I think that it is the student of arts (that English title which is as vague and unmeaning as the Scottish one of humanities)—student of ancient classical literature—who, whether man or woman, has least perception of the modern spirit or sympathy with the sorrows of the world. With all honour to the classical authors, there are two things in which they were deficient—the spirit of broad humanity and the sense of humour. All ancient literature is grave—nay, sad. It is also aristocratic for learning was the possession of the few. While writing this narrative I came upon a notable thing done by Miss Crystal Eastman, a member of the New York Bar, and Secretary of the State Commission on Employers' Liability. It is difficult for us to understand how so many good things are blocked, not only in the Federal Government, but in the separate States, by the written constitutions. In Great Britain the Constitution consists of unwritten principles embodied either in Parliamentary statutes or in the common law, and yields to any Act which Parliament may pass, and the judiciary can impose no veto on it. This is one reason why England is so far ahead of the United States in labour legislation. Miss Eastman was the principal speaker at the annual meeting in January, 1910, of the New York State Bar Association. She is a trained economic investigator as well as a lawyer, and her masterly analysis of conditions under the present liability law held close attention, and carried conviction to many present that a radical change was necessary. The recommendations for the statute were to make limited compensation for all accidents, except those wilfully caused by the victim, compulsory on all employers. With regard to dangerous occupations the person who profits by them should bear the greatest share of the loss through accident. As for the constitutionality of such legislation Miss Eastman said—"If our State Constitution cannot be interpreted so as to recognise such an idea of justice then I think we should amend our Constitution. I see no reason why we should stand in such awe of a document which expressly provides for its own revision every ten years." The evils against which this brave woman lawyer contends are real and grievous. Working people in America who suffer from injury are unmercifully exploited by the ambulance-chasing lawyers. Casualty insurance companies are said to be weary of being diverted from their regular business to become a mere fighting force in the Courts to prevent the injured or the dependents from getting any compensation. The long-suffering public is becoming aware that the taxpayers are compelled to bear the burden of supporting the pitifully great multitude of incapacitated or rendered dependent because of industrial accident or occupational diseases. Employers insure their liability, and the poor man has to fight an insurance company, and at present reform is blocked on the plea that it is unconstitutional. There are difficulties even in Australia, and to enquire into such difficulties would be good work for women lawyers.

CHAPTER XIV
SPECULATION, CHARITY, AND A BOOK

In the meantime my family history went on. My nephew was sent to the Northern Territory to take over the branch of the English and Scottish Bank at Palmerston, and he took his sister from school to go with him and stay three months in the tropics. He was only 21 at the time. Four years after he went to inspect the branch, and took his sister with him again. I think she loved Port Darwin more than he did, and she always stood up for the climate. South Australia did a great work in building, unaided by any other Australian State, the telegraph line from Port Darwin to Adelaide, and at one time it was believed that rich goldfields were to be opened in this great empty land, which the British Government had handed over to South Australia, because Stuart had been the first to cross the island continent, and the handful of South Australian colonists bad connected telegraphically the north and the south. The telegraph building had been contracted for by Darwent and Dalwood, and my brother, through the South Australian Bank, was helping to finance them. That was in 1876-7. This was the first, but not the last by any means, of enterprises which contractors were not able to carry out in this State, either from taking a big enterprise at too low a rate or from lack of financial backing. The Government, as in the recent cases of the Pinnaroo Railway and the Outer Harbour, had to complete the halfdone work as the direct employer of labour and the direct purchaser of materials. A great furore for goldmining in the Northern Territory arose, and people in England bought city allotments in Palmerston, which was expected to become the queen city of North Australia, Port Darwin is no whit behind Sydney Harbour in beauty and capacity. The navies of the world could ride safely in its waters. A railway of 150 miles in length, the first section of the great transcontinental line, which was to extend from Palmerston to Port Augusta, was built to connect Pine Creek, where there was gold to be found, with the seaboard. South Australia was more than ever a misnomer for this State. Victoria lay more to the south than our province, and now that we stretched far inside the tropics the name seemed ridiculous. My friend Miss Sinnett suggested Centralia as the appropriate name for the State, which by this gift was really the central State; but in the present crisis, when South Australia finds the task of keeping the Northern Territory white too arduous and too costly, and is offering it on handsome terms to the Commonwealth, Centralia might not continue to be appropriate. Our northern possession has cost South Australia much. The sums of money sunk in prospecting for gold and other metals have been enormous, and at present there are more Chinese there than Europeans. In the early days, when the Wrens were there, Eleanor was surprised when their wonderful Chinese cook came to her and said, "Missie, I go along a gaol tomorrow. You take Ah Kei. He do all light till I go out!" The cook had been tried and condemned for larceny, but he was allowed to retain his situation till the last hour. Instead of being kept in gaol pending his trial he earned his wages and did his work. He had no desire to escape. He liked Palmerston and the bank, and he went back to the latter when released. He was an incorrigible thief, and got into trouble again; but as a cook he was superlative.

That decade of the eighties was a most speculative time all over Australia and New Zealand. I was glad that leaving the English and Scottish Bank enabled my brother to go into political and official life, but it also allowed him to speculate far beyond what he could have done if he had been manager of a bank. Everybody speculated—in mines, in land, and in leases. I was earning by my pen a very decent income, and I spent it, sometimes wisely and sometimes foolishly. I could be liberal to church and to good causes. I was able to keep a dear little State child at school for two years after the regulation age, and I was amply repaid by seeing her afterwards an honoured wife and mother, able to assist her children and their companions with their lessons. I helped some lame dogs over the stile. One among them was a young American of brilliant scholastic attainments, who was the victim of hereditary alcoholism. His mother, a saintly and noble prohibitionist worker, whom I afterwards met in America, had heard of me, and wrote asking me to keep a watchful eye on her boy. This I did for about 12 months, and found him employment.

He held a science degree, and was an authority on mineralogy, metallurgy, and kindred subjects. During this speculative period he persuaded me to plunge (rather wildly for me) in mining shares. I plunged to the extent of 500 pounds, and I owe it to the good sense and practical ability of my nephew that I lost no more heavily than I did, for he paid 100 pounds to let me off my bargain.

My protege continued to visit me weekly, and we wrote to one another once a week or oftener. The books I lent to him I know to this day by their colour and the smell of tobacco. I wrote to his mother regularly, and consulted with his good friend, Mr. Waterhouse, over what was best to be done. One bad outburst he had when he had got some money through me to pay off liabilities. I recollect his penitent, despairing confession, with the reference to Edwin Arnold's poem

He who died at Azun gave

This to those who dug his grave.

The time came when I felt I could hold him no longer, although that escapade was forgiven, and I determined to send him to his mother—not without misgivings about what she might have still to suffer. He wrote to me occasionally. His health was never good, and I attribute the craving for drink and excitement a good deal to physical causes; but at the same time I am sure that he could have withstood it by a more resolute will. The will is the character—it is the real man. When people say that the first thing in education is to break the will, they make a radical mistake. Train the will to work according to the dictates of an enlightened conscience, for it is all we have to trust to for the stability of character. My poor lad called me his Australian mother. When I saw his real mother, I wondered more and more what sort of a husband she had, or what atavism Edward drew from to produce a character so unlike hers. I heard nothing from herself of what she went through, but from her friends I gathered that he had several outbreaks, and cost her far more than she could afford. She paid everything that he owed in Adelaide, except her debt to me, but that I was repaid after her death in 1905, and she always felt that I had been a true friend to her wayward son. I recollect one day my friend coming on his weekly visit with a face of woe to tell me he had seen a man in dirt and rags, with half a shirt, who had been well acquainted with Charles Dickens and other notables in London. My friend had fed him and clothed him, but he wanted to return to England to rich friends. I wrote to a few good folk, and we raised the money and sent the wastrel to the old country. How grateful he appeared to be, especially to the kind people who had taken him in; but he never wrote a line. We never heard from him again. Years afterwards I wrote to his brother-in-law, asking where the object of our charity now was, if he were still alive. The reply was that his ingratitude did not surprise the writer—that he was a hopeless drunkard, a remittance man, whom the family had to ship off as soon as possible when our ill-judged kindness sent him to England. At that time he was in Canada, but it was not worth while to give any address. When Mr. Bowyear started the Charity Organization Society in Adelaide, he said I was no good as a visitor; I was too credulous, and had not half enough of the detective in me. But I had not much faith in this remittance man.

I have been strongly tempted to omit altogether the next book which I wrote; but, as this is to be a sincere narrative of my life and its work, I must pierce the veil of anonymity and own up to "An Agnostic's Progress." I had been impressed with the very different difficulties the soul of man has to encounter nowadays from those so triumphantly overcome by Christian in the great work of John Bunyan in the first part of "The Pilgrim's Progress." He cannot now get out of the Slough of Despond by planting his foot on the stepping stones of the Promiscs. He cannot, like Hopeful, pluck from his bosom the Key of Promise which opens every lock in Doubting Castle when the two pilgrims are shut in it by Giant Despair, when they are caught trespassing on his grounds. Even assured Christians, we know, may occasionally trespass on these grounds of doubt; but the weapons of modern warfare are not of the seventeenth century. The Interpreter's House in the old allegory dealt only with things found in the Bible, the only channel of revelation to John Bunyan. To the modern pilgrim God reveals Himself in Nature, in art, in literature, and in history. The Interpreter's Hand had to do with all these things. Vanity Fair is not a place through which all pilgrims must pass as quickly as possible, shutting their eyes and stopping their ears so that they should neither see nor hear the wicked things that are done and said there. Vanity Fair is the world in which we all have to live and do our work well, or neglect it. Pope and Pagan are not the old giants who used to devour pilgrims, but who can now only gnash their teeth at them in impotent rage. They are live forces, quite active, and with agents and supporters alert to capture souls. Of all the influences which affected for evil my young life I perhaps resented most Mrs. Sherwood's "Infant's Progress." There were three children in it going from the City of Destruction to the Celestial City by the route laid down by John Bunyan; but they were handicapped even more severely than the good Christian himself with his heavy burden—for that fell off his back at the first sight of the Cross and Him who was nailed to it, accepted by the eye of Faith as the one Sacrifice for the sins of the world—for the three little ones, Humble Mind, Playful, and Peace, were accompanied always and everywhere by an imp called Inbred Sin, who never ceased to tempt them to evil.

The doctrine of innate human depravity is one of the most paralysing dogmas that human fear invented or priestcraft encouraged. I did not think of publishing "An Agnostic's Progress" at first. I wrote it to relieve my own mind. I wanted to satisfy myself that reverent agnostics were by no means materialists; that man's nature might or might not be consciously immortal, but it was spiritual; that in the duties which lay before each of us towards ourselves and towards our fellow-creatures, there was scope for spiritual energy and spiritual emotion. I was penetrated by Browning's great idea expressed over and over again—the expansion of Paul's dictum that faith is not certainty, but a belief without sufficient proof, a belief which leads to right action and to self-sacrifice. Of the 70 years of life which one might hope to live and work in, I had no mean idea. I asked in the newspaper, "Is life so short?" and answered. "No." I expanded and spiritualized the idea in a sermon, and I again answered emphatically "No." I saw the continuation and the expansion of true ideas by succeeding generations. To the question put sometimes peevishly, "Is life worth living?" I replied with equal emphasis, "Yes." My mother told me of old times. I recalled half a century of progress, and I hoped the forward movement would continue. I read the manuscript of "An Agnostic's Progress" to Mr. and Mrs. Barr Smith, and they thought so well of it that they offered to take it to England on one of their many visits to the old country, where they had no doubt it would find a publisher. Trubner's reader reported most favourably of the book, and we thought there was an immediate prospect of its publication; but Mr. Trubner died, and the matter was not taken up by his successor, and my friends did what I had expressly said they were not to do, and had it printed and published at their own expense. There were many printer's errors in it, but it was on the whole well reviewed, though it did not sell well. The Spectator joined issue with me on the point that it is only through the wicket gate of Doubt that we can come to any faith that is of value; but I am satisfied that I took the right stand there. My mother was in no way disquieted or disturbed by my writing the book, and few of my friends read it or knew about it. I still appeared so engrossed with work on The Register and The Observer that my time was quite well enough accounted for. I tried for a prize of 100 pounds offered by The Sydney Mail with a novel called "Handfasted," but was not successful, for the judge feared that it was calculated to loosen the marriage tie—it was too socialistic and consequently dangerous.

CHAPTER XV
JOURNALISM AND POLITICS

In reviewing books I took the keenest Interest in the "Carlyle Biographies and Letters," because my mother recollected Jeanie Welch as a child, and her father was called in always for my grandfather Brodie's illnesses. I was also absorbed in the "Life and Letters of George Eliot." The Barr Smiths gave me the "Life and Letters of Balzac," and many of his books in French, which led me to write both for The Register and for The Melbourne Review. I also wrote "A last word," which was lost by The Centennial in Sydney when it died out. It was also from Mrs. Barr Smith that I got so many of the works of Alphonse Daudet in French, which enabled me to give a rejoinder to Marcus Clark's assertion that Balzac was a French Dickens. Indeed, looking through my shelves, I see so many books which suggested articles and criticisms which were her gifts that I always connect her with my journalistic career.

Many people have consulted me about publishing poems, novels, and essays. As I was known to have actually got books published in England, and to be a professional journalist and reviewer, I dare say some of those who applied to me for encouragement thought I was actuated by literary jealousy; but people are apt to think they have a plot when they have only an incident, or two or three incidents; and many who can write clever and even brilliant letters have no idea of the construction of a story that will arrest and sustain the reader's attention. The people who consulted me all wanted money for their work. They had such excellent uses for money. They had too little. They were neither willing nor able to bear the cost of publication, and it was absolutely necessary that their work should be good enough for a business man to undertake it. I am often surprised that I found English publishers myself, and the handicap of distance and other things is even greater now. If stories are excessively Australian, they lose the sympathies of the bulk of the public. If they are mildly Australian, the work is thought to lack distinctiveness.

Great genius can overcome these things, but great genius is rare everywhere. Except for my friend Miss Mackay (Mrs. F. Martin), I know no Australian novelist of genius, and her work is only too rare in fiction. Mrs. Cross reaches her highest level in "The Masked Man." but she does not keep it up, though she writes well and pleasantly. Of course poetry does not pay anywhere until a great reputation is made. Poetry must be its own exceeding great reward. And yet I agree with Charles Kingsley that if you wish to cultivate a really good prose style you should begin with verse. In my teens I wrote rhymes and tried to write sonnets. I encouraged writing games among my young people, and it is surprising how much cleverness could be developed. I can write verses with ease, but very rarely could I rise to poetry; and therefore I fear I was not encouraging to the budding Australian poet.

There was a column quite outside of The Register to which I liked to contribute for love. That was "The Riddler," which appeared in The Observer and in The Evening Journal on Saturdays. It brought me in contact with Mr. William Holden, long the oldest journalist in South Australia, who revelled in statistical returns and algebraical problems and earth measurements, but who also appreciated a good charade or double acrostic. I used to give some of the ingredients for his "Christmas Mince Pie," and wrote many riddles of various sorts. My charades were not so elegant as some arranged by Miss Clark, and not so easily found out; and my double acrostics were not so subtle as those given in competition nowadays, but they were in the eighties reckoned excellent. My fame had reached the ears of Mrs. Alfred Watts (nee Giles), who spent her early colonial life on Kangaroo Island, and she asked me to write some double acrostics for the poor incurables. I stared at her in amazement. "We want to be quite well to tackle double acrostics and to have access to books. Does not Punch speak of the titled lady, eager to win a guinea prize, who gave seven volumes of Carlyle's works to seven upper servants, and asked each to search one to find a certain quotation?" "Oh," said Mrs. Watts, "I don't mean for the incurables to amuse themselves with. I mean for the benefit of the home."

In the end I prepared a book of charades and double acrostics, for the printing and binding of which Mrs. Watts paid. It was entitled "Silver Wattle," and the proceeds from the sale of this little book went to help the funds of the home. For a second volume issued for the same purpose Mrs. Strawbridge wrote some poems, Mrs. H. M. Davidson a translation of Victor Huge, Miss Clark her beautiful "Flowers of Greece," and her niece some pretty verses, which, combined with the double acrostics, and acting charades supplied by me, made an attractive volume. Mrs. Watts had something of a literary turn, which found expression in "Memories of Early Days in South Australia," a book printed for private circulation among her family and intimate friends. Dealing with the years between 1837 and 1845 it was very interesting to old colonists, particularly when they were able to identify the people mentioned, sometimes by initials and sometimes by pseudonyms. The author was herself an incurable invalid from an accident shortly after her marriage, and felt keenly for all the inmates of the Fullarton Home.

In 1877 my brother John—with whom I had never quarrelled in my life, and who helped and encouraged me in everything that I did—retired from the English, Scottish, and Australian Bank, and decided to contest a seat for the Legislative Council. It was the last occasion on which the Council was elected with the State as one district. Although he announced his candidature only the night before nomination day, and did not address a single meeting, he was elected third on the poll. He afterwards became the Chief Secretary, and later Commissioner of Public Works. He was an excellent worker on committees, and was full of ideas and suggestions. Although not a good speaker, he rejoiced in my standing on platform or in pulpit. He was nearly as democratic as I was; and when he invented the phrase "effective voting" it was from the sense that true democracy demanded not merely a chance, but a certainty, that the vote given at the poll should be effective for some one. My brother David inherited all the Conservatism of the Brodies for generations back. Greatly interested in all abstruse problems and abstract questions he had various schemes for the regeneration of mankind. Two opposing theories concerning the working of bi-cameral Legislatures supplied me with material for a Review article. One theory was intensely Conservative, and emanated from my brother David, who was a poor man. The other was held by the richest man of my acquaintance, and was distinctly Liberal. My brother argued that the Upper House should have the power to tax its own constituents, and was utterly opposed to any extension of the franchise. My rich friend objected to the limited franchise, and desired to have the State proclaimed one electorate with proportional representation as a safeguard against unwise legislation and as a means to assist reforms. The great blot, he considered, on Australian Constitutions was the representation by districts, especially for the House that controlled the public purse. If districts were to be tolerated at all, they should be represented by men who had a longer tenure of office than our Assembly's three years, and who did not have so often to ask for votes, which frequently depended on a railway or a jetty or a Rabbit Bill. So long as a Government depends for its existence on the support of local representatives it is tempted to spend public money to gratify them. Both men were Freetraders, and both believed strongly in the justice of land values taxation.

My friend the late Professor Pearson had entered into active political life in Melbourne, and was a regular writer for The Age. Perhaps no other man underwent more obloquy from his old friends for taking the side of Graham Berry, especially as he was a Freetrader, and the popular party was Protectionist. He justified his action by saying that a mistake in the fiscal policy of a country should not prevent a real Democrat from siding with the party which opposed monopoly, especially in land. He saw in "LATIFUNDIA"—huge estates—the ruin of the Roman Empire, and its prevalence in the United Kingdom was the greatest danger ahead of it. In these young countries the tendency to build up large holdings was naturally fostered by what was the earliest of our industries. Sheepfarming is not greatly pursued in the United States or Canada, because of the rigorous winter—but Australia is the favourite home of the merino sheep. Originally there was no need to buy land, or even to pay rent to the Government for it; the land had no value till settlement gave it. The squatter leased it on easy terms, and bought it only when it had sufficient value to be desired by agriculturists or by selectors who posed as agriculturists. When he bought it he generally complained of the price these selectors compelled him to pay, but it was then secure; and, with the growth of population and the railroads and other improvements, these enforced purchasers, even in 1877, had built up vast estates in single hands in every State in Australia. In The Melbourne Review for April, 1877, Professor Pearson sketched a plan of land taxation, which was afterwards carried out, in which the area of land held was the test for graduated taxation. Henry George had not then declared his gospel; and, although I felt that there was something very faulty in the scheme, I did not declare in my article on the subject that an acre in Collins street might be of more value than 50,000 acres of pastoral land 500 miles from the seaboard, and was therefore more fitly liable to taxation for the advantage of the whole community, who had given to that acre this exceptional value. I did not declare it because I did not believe it. But I thought that the end aimed at—the breaking up of large estates—could be better and more safely effected, though not so quickly, by a change in the incidence of succession duties.

Some time after I saw a single copy of Henry George's "Progress and Poverty" on Robertson's shelves, and bought it, and it was I who after reading this book opened in the three most important Australian colonies the question of the taxation of land values. An article I wrote went into The Register, and Mr. Liston, of Kapunda, read it, and spoke of it at a farmers' meeting. I had then a commission from The Sydney Morning Herald to write on any important subject, and I wrote on this. It appeared, like a previous article on Howell's "Conflicts of Capital and Labour," as an unsigned article. A new review, The Victorian, had been started by Mortimer Franlyn, which paid contributors; and, now that I was a professional journalist, I thought myself entitled to ask remuneration. I sent to the new periodical, published in Melbourne, a fuller treatment of the book than had been given to the two newspapers, under the title of "A Californian Political Economist." This fell into the hands of Henry George himself, in a reading room in San Francisco, and he wrote an acknowledgment of it to me. In South Australia the first tax on unimproved land values was imposed. It was small—only a halfpenny in the pound, but without any exemption; and its imposition was encouraged by the fact that we had had bad seasons and a falling revenue. The income tax in England was originally a war tax, and they say that if there is not a war the United States will never be able to impose an income tax. The separate States have not the power to impose such a tax. Henry George said to me in his home in New York:— "I wonder at you, with your zeal and enthusiasm, and your power of speaking, devoting yourself to such a small matter as proportional representation, when you see the great land question before you." I replied that to me it was not a small matter. I cannot, however, write my autobiography without giving prominence to the fact that I was the pioneer in Australia in this as in the other matter of proportional representation.

CHAPTER XVI
SORROW AND CHANGE

In the long and cheerful life of my dear mother there at last came a change. At 94 she fell and broke her wrist. The local doctor (a stranger), who was called in, not knowing her wonderful constitution, was averse from setting the wrist, and said that she would never be able to use the hand. But I insisted, and in six, weeks she was able to resume her knitting, and never felt any ill effects. At 95 she had a fall, apparently without cause, and was never able to stand again. She had to stay in bed for the last 13 months of her life, with a gradual decay of the faculties which had previously been so keen. My mother wanted me with her always. Her talk was all of times far back in her life—not of Melrose, where she had lived for 25 years, but of Scoryhall (pronounced Scole), where she had lived as a girl. I had been shown through the house by my aunt Handyside in 1865, and I could follow her mind wanderings and answer her questions. As she suffered so little pain it was difficult for my mother to realize the seriousness of her illness; and, tiring of her bedroom, she begged to be taken to the study, where, with her reading and knitting, she had spent so many happy hours while I did my writing. Delighted though she was at the change, a return to her bed—as to all invalids—was a comfort, and she never left it again. Miss Goodham—an English nurse and a charming woman, who has since remained a friend and correspondent of the family—was sent to help us for a few days at the last. Another sorrow came to us at this time in the loss of my ward's husband, and Rose Hood—nee Duval—returned to live near me with her three small children. Her commercial training enabled her to take a position as clerk in the State Children's Department, which she retained until her death. The little ones were very sweet and good, but the supervision of them during the day added a somewhat heavy responsibility to our already overburdened household. In these days, when one hears so much of the worthlessness of servants, it is a joy to remember how our faithful maid—we kept only one for that large house—at her own request, did all the laundry work for the family of five, and all through the three years of Eleanor's illness waited on her with untiring devotion.

An amusing episode which would have delighted the heart of my dear friend Judge Lindsay occurred about this time. The fruit from our orange trees which grew along the wall bordering an adjoining paddock was an irresistible temptation to wandering juveniles, and many and grievous were the depredations. Patience, long drawn out, at last gave way, and when the milkman caught two delinquents one Saturday afternoon with bulging blouses of forbidden fruit it became necessary to make an example of some one. The trouble was to devise a fitting punishment. A Police Court, I had always maintained, was no place for children; corporal punishment was out of the question; and the culprits stood tremblingly awaiting their fate till a young doctor present suggested a dose of Gregory's powder. His lawyer friend acquiesced, and Gregory's powder it was. A moment's hesitation and the nauseous draught was swallowed to the accompaniment of openly expressed sympathy, one dear old lady remarking, "Poor children and not so much as a taste of sugar." Probably, however, the unkindest cut of all was the carrying away by the milkman of the stolen fruit! The cure was swift and effective; and ever after the youth of the district, like the Pharisee of old, passed by on the other side.

My dear mother died about 8 o'clock on the evening of December 8, 1887, quietly and painlessly. With her death, which was an exceedingly great loss to me, practically ended my quiet life of literary work. Henceforth I was free to devote my efforts to the fuller public work for which I had so often longed, but which my mother's devotion to and dependence on me rendered impossible. But I missed her untiring sympathy, for with all her love for the old days and the old friends there was no movement for the advancement of her adopted land that did not claim her devoted attention. But though I was now free to take up public work, the long strain of my mother's illness and death had affected my usually robust health, and I took things quietly. I had been asked by the University Shakspeare Society to give a lecture on

Donnelly's book, "The Great Cryptogram;" or "Who Wrote Shakspeare's Plays?" and it was prepared during this period, and has frequently been delivered since. October of the year following my mothers death found me again in Melbourne, where I rejoiced in the renewal of a friendship with Mr. and Mrs. Thomas Walker, the former of whom had been connected with the construction of the overland railway. They were delightful literary people, and I had met them at the hospitable house of the Barr-Smiths, and been introduced as "a literary lady." "Then perhaps," said Mr. Walker, "you can give us the information we have long sought in vain—who wrote 'Clara Morrison?'" Their surprise at my "I did" was equalled by the pleasure I felt at their kind appreciation of my book, and that meeting was the foundation of a lifelong friendship. Before my visit closed I was summoned to Gippsland through the death by accident of my dear sister Jessie—the widow of Andrew Murray, once editor of The Argus—and the year 1888 ended as sadly for me as the previous one had done. The following year saw the marriage of my nephew, Charles Wren of the E.S. and A. Bank, to Miss Hall, of Melbourne. On his deciding to live on in the old home, I, with Ellen Gregory, whom I had brought out in 1867 to reside with relations, but who has remained to be the prop and mainstay of my old age—and Mrs. Hood and her three children, moved to a smaller and more suitable house I had in another part of East Adelaide. A placid flowing of the river of life for a year or two led on to my being elected, in 1892, President of the Girls' Literary Society. This position I filled with joy to myself and, I hope, with advantage to others, until some years later the society ceased to exist.

Crowded and interesting as my life had been hitherto, the best was yet to be. My realization of Browning's beautiful line from "Rabbi Ben Ezra"—"The last of life, for which the first was made," came when I saw opening before me possibilities for public service undreamed of in my earlier years. For the advancement of effective voting I had so far confined my efforts to the newspapers. My brother John had suggested the change of name from proportional representation to effective voting as one more likely to catch the popular ear, and I had proposed a modification of Hare's original plan of having one huge electorate, and suggested instead the adoption of six-member districts. The State as one electorate returning 42 members for the Assembly may be magnificent, and may also be the pure essence of democracy, but it is neither commonsense nor practicable. "Why not take effective voting to the people?" was suggested to me. No sooner said than done. I had ballot papers prepared and leaflets printed, and I began the public campaign which has gone on ever since. During a visit to Melbourne as a member of a charities conference it was first discovered that I had some of the gifts of a public speaker. My friend, the Rev. Charles Strong, had invited me to lecture before his working men's club at Collingwood, and I chose as my subject "Effective Voting."

When on my return Mr. Barr Smith, who had long grasped the principle of justice underlying effective voting, and was eager for its adoption, offered to finance a lecturing tour through the State, I jumped at the offer. There was the opportunity for which I had been waiting for years. I got up at unearthly hours to catch trains, and sometimes succeeded only through the timely lifts of kindly drivers. Once I went in a carrier's van, because I had missed the early morning cars. I travelled thousands of miles in all weathers to carry to the people the gospel of electoral reform. Disappointments were frequent, and sometimes disheartening; but the silver lining of every cloud turned up somewhere, and I look back on that first lecturing tour as a time of the sowing of good seed, the harvest of which is now beginning to ripen. I had no advance agents to announce my arrival, and at one town in the north I found nobody at the station to meet me. I spent the most miserable two and a half hours of my life waiting Micawber-like for something to turn up; and it turned up in the person of the village blacksmith. I spoke to him, and explained my mission to the town. He had heard nothing of any meeting. Incidentally I discovered that my correspondent was in Adelaide, and had evidently forgotten all about my coming. "Well," I said to the blacksmith, "if you can get together a dozen intelligent men I will explain effective voting to them." He looked at me with a dumbfounded air, and then burst out, "Good G—, madam, there are not three intelligent men in the town." But the old order has changed, and in 1909 Mrs. Young addressed an enthusiastic audience of 150 in the same town and on the same subject. The town, moreover, is in a Parliamentary district, in which every candidate at the recent general election—and there were seven of them—supported effective voting. Far down in the south I went to a little village containing seven churches, which accounted (said the local doctor) for the extreme backwardness of its inhabitants. "They have so many church affairs to attend to that there is no time to think of anything else." At the close of this lecturing tour The Register undertook the public count through its columns, which did so much to bring the reform before the people of South Australia. Public interest was well aroused on the matter before my long projected trip to America took shape. "Come and teach us how to vote," my American friends had been writing to me for years; but I felt that it was a big order for a little woman of 68 to undertake the conversion to electoral reform of 60 millions of the most conceited people in the world. Still I went. I left Adelaide bound for America on April 4, 1893, as a Government Commissioner and delegate to the Great World's Fair Congresses in Chicago.

In Melbourne and Sydney on my way to the boat for San Francisco I found work to do. Melbourne was in the throes of the great financial panic, when bank after bank closed its doors; but the people went to church as usual. I preached in the Unitarian Church on the Sunday, and lectured in Dr. Strong's Australian Church on Monday. In Sydney Miss Rose Scott had arranged a drawing-room meeting for a lecture on effective voting. A strong convert I made on that occasion was Mr. (afterwards Sr.) Walker. A few delightful hours I spent at his charming house on the harbour with his family, and was taken by them to see many beauty spots. Those last delightful days in Sydney left me with pleasant Australian memories to carry over the Pacific. When the boat sailed on April 17, the rain came down in torrents. Some interesting missionaries were on board. One of them, the venerable Dr. Brown, who had been for 30 years labouring in the Pacific, introduced me to Sir John Thurston. Mr. Newell was returning to Samoa after a two years' holiday in England. He talked much, and well about his work. He had 104 students to whom he was returning. He explained that they became missionaries to other more benighted and less civilized islands, where their knowledge of the traditions and customs of South Sea Islanders made them invaluable as propagandists. The writings of Robert Louis Stevenson, had prepared me to find in the Samoans a handsome and stalwart race, with many amiable traits, and I was not disappointed. The beauty of the scenery appealed to me strongly, and I doubt whether "the light that never was on sea or land" could have rivalled the magic charm of the one sunrise we saw at Samoa. During the voyage I managed to get in one lecture, and many talks on effective voting. Had I been superstitious my arrival in San Francisco on Friday, May 12, might have boded ill for the success of my mission, but I was no sooner ashore than my friend Alfred Cridge took me in charge, and the first few days were a whirl of meetings, addresses and interviews.

CHAPTER XVII
IMPRESSIONS OF AMERICA

Alfred Cridge, who reminded me so much of my brother David that I felt at home with him immediately, had prepared the way for my lectures on effective voting in San Francisco. He was an even greater enthusiast than I. "America needs the reform more than Australia," he used to say. But if America needs effective voting to check corruption, Australia needs it just as much to prevent the degradation of political life in the Commonwealth and States to the level of American politics. My lectures in San Francisco, as elsewhere in America, were well attended, and even better received. Party politics had crushed out the best elements of political life, and to be independent of either party gave a candidate, as an agent told Judge Lindsay when he was contesting the governorship of Colorado, "as much chance as a snowball would have in hell." So that reformers everywhere were eager to hear of a system of voting that would free the electors from the tyranny of parties, and at the same time render a candidate independent of the votes of heckling minorities, and dependent only on the votes of the men who believed in him and his politics. I met men and women interested in public affairs—some of them well known, others most worthy to be known, and all willing to lend the weight of their character and intelligence to the betterment of human conditions at home and abroad. Among these were Judge Maguire, a leader of the Bar in San Francisco and a member of the State Legislature, who had fought trusts, "grafters," and "boodlers" through the whole of his public career, and Mr. James Barry, proprietor of The Star.

"You come from Australia, the home of the secret ballot?" was the greeting I often received, and that really was my passport to the hearts of reformers all over America. From all sides I heard that it was to the energy and zeal of the Singletaxers in the various States—a well-organized and compact body—that the adoption of the secret ballot was due. To that celebrated journalist, poetess, and economic writer, Charlotte Perkins Stetson, who was a cultured Bostonian, living in San Francisco, I owed one of the best women's meetings I ever addressed. The subject was "State children and the compulsory clauses in our Education Act," and everywhere in the States people were interested in the splendid work of our State Children's Department and educational methods. Intelligence and not wealth I found to be the passport to social life among the Americans I met. At a social evening ladies as well as their escorts were expected to remove bonnets and mantles in the hall, instead of being invited into a private room as in Australia—a custom I thought curious until usage made it familiar. The homeliness and unostentatiousness of the middle class American were captivating. My interests have always been in people and in the things that make for human happiness or misery rather than in the beauties of Nature, art, or architecture. I want to know how the people live, what wages are, what the amount of comfort they can buy; how the people are fed, taught, and amused; how the burden of taxation falls; how justice is executed; how much or how little liberty the people enjoy. And these things I learned to a great extent from my social intercourse with those cultured reformers of America. Among these people I had not the depressing feeling of immensity and hugeness which marred my enjoyment when I arrived at New York. My literary lectures on the Brownings and George Eliot were much appreciated, especially in the East, where I found paying audiences in the fall or autumn of the year. These lectures have been delivered many times in Australia; and, as the result of the Browning lecture given in the Unitarian Schoolroom in Wakefield street, Adelaide, I received from the pen of Mr. J. B. Mather a clever epigram. The room was large and sparsely filled, and to the modest back seat taken by my friend my voice scarcely penetrated. So he amused himself and me by writing:

> I have no doubt that words of sense
>
> Are falling from the lips of Spence.
>
> Alas! that Echo should be drowning
>
> Both words of Spence and sense of Browning.

I found the Brownings far better appreciated in America than in England, especially by American women. In spite of the fact that The San Francisco Chronicle had interviewed me favourably on my arrival, and that I knew personally some of the leading people on The Examiner, neither paper would report my lectures on effective voting. The Star, however, quite made up for the deficiencies of the other papers, and did all it could to help me and the cause. While in San Francisco I wrote an essay on "Electoral Reform" for a Toronto competition, in which the first prize was $500. Mr. Cridge was also a competitor; but, although many essays were sent in, for some reason the prize was never awarded, and we had our trouble for nothing. On my way to Chicago I stayed at a mining town to lecture on effective voting. I found the hostess of the tiny hotel a brilliant pianist and a perfect linguist, and she quoted poetry—her own and other people's—by the yard. A lady I journeyed with told me that she had been travelling for seven years with her husband and "Chambers's Encyclopedia." I thought they used the encyclopaedia as a guide book until, in a sort of postscript to our conversation, I discovered the husband to be a book agent, better known in America as a "book fiend."

Nobody had ever seen anything like the World's Fair. My friend Dr. Bayard Holmes of Chigago, whose acquaintance I made through missing a suburban train, expressed a common feeling when he said he could weep at the thought that it was all to be destroyed—that the creation evolved from the best brains of America should be dissolved. Much of our human toil is lost and wasted, and much of our work is more ephemeral than we think; but this was a conscious creation of hundreds of beautiful buildings for a six months' existence. Nowhere else except in America could the thing have been done, and nowhere else in America but in Chicago. At the Congress of Charity and correction I found every one interested in Australia's work for destitute children. It was difficult for Miss Windeyer, of Sydney, and myself—the only Australians present—to put ourselves in the place of many who believed in institutions where children of low physique, low morals, and low intelligence are massed together, fed, washed, drilled, taught by rule, never individualized, and never mothered. I spoke from pulpits in Chicago and Indianapolis on the subject, and was urged to plead with the Governor of the latter State to use his influence to have at least tiny mites of six years of age removed from the reformatory, which was under the very walls of the gaol. But he was obdurate to my pleadings and arguments, as he had been to those of the State workers. He maintained that these tiny waifs of six were incorrigible, and were better in institutions than in homes. The most interesting woman I met at the conference was the Rev. Mrs. Anna Garlin Spencer, pastor of Bell Street Chapel, Providence. I visited her at home, in that retreat of Baptists, Quakers, and others from the hard persecution of the New England Orthodoxy, the founders of which had left England in search of freedom to worship God. Her husband was the Unitarian minister of another congregation in the same town. At the meetings arranged by Mrs. Spencer, Professor Andrews, one of the Behring Sea arbitrators, and Professor Wilson were present; and they invited me to speak on effective voting at the Brunn University.

In Philadelphia I addressed seven meetings on the same subject. At six of them an editor of a little reform paper was present. For two years he had lived on brown bread and dried apples, in order that he could save enough to buy a newspaper plant for the advocacy of reforms. In his little paper he replied to the critics, who assured me that it was no use worrying, as everything would come right in time. "Time only brings wonders," he wrote, "when good and great men and women rise up to move the world along. Time itself brings only decay and death. The truth is 'Nothing will come right unless those who feel they have the truth speak, and Work, and strain as if on them alone rested the destinies of the world.'" I went to see a celebrated man, George W. Childs, who had made a fortune out of The Philadelphia Ledger, and who was one of the best employers in the States. He knew everybody, not only in America but in Europe; and his room was a museum of gifts from great folks all over the world. But, best of all, he, with his devoted friend Anthony Drexel, had founded the Drexel Institute, which was their magnificent educational legacy to the historic town. I saw the Liberty Bell in Chicago—the bell that rang out the Declaration of Independence, and cracked soon after—which is cherished by all good Americans. It had had a triumphant progress to and from the

World's Fair, and I was present when once again it was safely landed in Independence Hall, Philadelphia. I think the Americans liked me, because I thought their traditions reputably old, and did not, like European visitors, call everything crude and new. The great war in America strengthened the Federal bond, while it loosened the attachment to the special Satte in which the United States citizen lives. Railroads and telegraphs have done much to make Americans homogeneous, and the school system grapples bravely with the greater task of Americanizing the children of foreigners, who arrive in such vast numbers. Canada allowed the inhabitants of lower Canada to keep their language, their laws, and their denominational schools; and the consequence is that these Canadian-British subjects are more French than the French, more conservative than the Tories, and more Catholic than Irish or Italians. Education is absolutely free in America up to the age of 18; but I never heard an American complain of being taxed to educate other people's children. In Auburn I met Harriet Tribman, called the "Moses of her people"—an old black woman who could neither read nor write, but who had escaped from slavery when young, and had made 19 journeys south, and been instrumental in the escape of 300 slaves. To listen to her was to be transferred to the pages of "Uncle Tom's Cabin." Her language was just that of Tom and old Jeff. A pious Christian, she was full of good works still. Her shanty was a refuge for the sick, blind, and maimed of her own people. I went all over Harvard University under the guidance of Professor Ashley, to whom our Chief Justice had given me a letter of introduction. He got up a drawing-room meeting for me, at which I met Dr. Gordon Ames, pastor of the Unitarian Church of the Disciples. He invited me to preach his thanksgiving service for him on the following Thursday, which I was delighted to do. Mrs. Ames was the factory inspector of women and children in Massachusetts, and was probably the wisest woman I met in my travels. She spoke to me of the evils of stimulating the religious sentiment too young, and said that the hushed awe with which most people spoke of God and His constant presence filled a child's mind with fear.

She related an experience with her own child, who on going to bed had asked if God was in the room. The child was told that God was always besides us. After being left in darkness the child was heard sobbing, and a return to the nursery elicited the confession, "Oh, mamma, I can't bear to be left with no one but God." Better the simple anthropomorphism which makes God like the good father, the generous uncle, the indulgent grandfather, or the strong elder brother.

Such ideas as these of God were held by the heroines of the following stories:—A little girl, a niece of the beloved Bishop Brooks, had done wrong, and was told to confess her sin to God before she slept, and to beg His forgiveness. When asked next day whether she had obeyed the command, she said—"Oh, yes! I told God all about it, and God said, 'Don't mention it, Miss Brooks.'" A similar injunction was laid upon a child brought up by a very severe and rather unjust aunt. Her reply when asked if she had confessed her sin was "I told God what I had done, and what you thought about it, and I just left it to Him." The response of a third American girl (who was somewhat of a "pickle" and had been reared among a number of boys) to the enquiry whether she had asked forgiveness for a wrong done was—"Oh, yes; I told God exactly what I had done, and He said, 'Great Scot, Elsie Murray, I know 500 little girls worse than you.'" To me this was a much healthier state of mind than setting children weeping for their sins, as I have done myself.

On my second visit to Boston I spent three weeks with the family of William, Lloyd Garrison, son of the famous Abolitionist. The Chief Justice had given me a letter of introduction to him, and I found him a true-hearted humanitarian, as devoted to the gospel of single tax as his father had been to that of anti-slavery. They lived in a beautiful house in Brookline, on a terrace built by an enterprising man who had made his money in New South Wales. Forty-two houses were perfectly and equally warmed by one great furnace, and all the public rooms of the ground floor, dining, and drawing rooms, library, and hall were connected by folding doors, nearly always open, which gave a feeling of space I never experienced elsewhere. Electric lighting and bells all over the house, hot and cold baths, lifts, the most complete laundry arrangements, and cupboards everywhere ensured the maximum of comfort with the minimum of labour. But in this house I began to be a little ashamed of being so narrow in my views on the coloured question. Mr. Garrison, animated with the spirit of the true brotherhood of man, was an advocate of the heathen Chinee, and was continually speaking of the goodness of the negro and coloured and yellow races, and of the injustice and rapacity of the white Caucasians. I saw the files of his father's paper, The Liberator, from its beginning in 1831 till its close, when the victory was won in 1865. Of the time spent in the Lloyd-Garrison household "nothing now is left but a majestic memory," which has been kept green by the periodical letters received from this noble man up till the time of his death last year. He showed me the monument erected to the memory of his father in Boston in the town where years before the great abolitionist had been stoned by the mob. Only recently it rejoiced my heart to know that a memorial to Lloyd Garrison the younger had been unveiled in Boston, his native city; at the same time that a similar honour was paid to his venerated leader, "the prophet of San Francisco."

I account it one of the greatest privileges of my visit to America that Mrs. Garrison introduced me to Oliver Wendell Holmes, and by appointment I had an hour and a half's chat with him in the last year of his long life. He was the only survivor of a famous band of New England writers, Longfellow, Emerson, Hawthorn, Bryant, Lowell, Whittier, and Whitman were dead. His memory was failing, and he forgot some of his own characters; but Elsie Venner he remembered perfectly and he woke to full animation when I objected to the fatalism of heredity as being about as paralysing to effort as the fatalism of Calvinism. As a medical man (and we are apt to forget the physician in the author) he took strong views of heredity. As a worker among our destitute children, I considered environment the greater factor of the two, and spoke of children of the most worthless parents who had turned out well when placed early in respectable and kindly homes. Before I left, the author presented me with an autograph copy of one of his books—a much-prized gift. He was reading Cotton Mather's "Memorabilia," not for theology, but for gossip. It was the only chronicle of the small beer of current events in the days of the witch persecutions, and the expulsion of the Quakers,

Baptists, and other schismatics. I have often felt proud that of all the famous men I have mentioned in this connection there was only one not a Unitarian, and that was Whittier, the Quaker poet of abolition; and his theology was of the mildest.

Another notable man with whom I had three hours' talk was Charles Dudley Warner, the humorous writer. I am not partial to American humorists generally, but the delicate and subtle humour of Dudley Warner I always appreciated. In our talk I saw his serious side, for he was keen on introducing the indeterminate sentence into his own State, on the lines of the Elmira and Concord Reformatories. He told me that he never talked in train: but during the three hours' journey to New York neither of us opened the books with which we had provided ourselves, and we each talked of our separate interests, and enjoyed the talk right through. Mrs. Harriet Beecher Stowe I saw, but her memory was completely gone. With Julia Ward Howe, the writer of "The Battle Hymn of the Republic" I spent a happy time. She had been the President of the New England Women's Club for 25 years, and was a charming and interesting woman. I was said to be very like her, and, indeed was often accosted by her name; but I think probably the reason was partly my cap, for Howe always wears one, and few other American ladies do. Whenever I was with her I was haunted by the beautiful lines from the closing verse of the "Battle Hymn"—

> In the beauty of the lilies, Christ was born, across the sea,
>
> With a glory in His bosom that transfigures you and me;
>
> As He died to make men holy, let us die to make men free,
>
> While God is marching on.

At her house I met many distinguished women. Mrs. J. F. Fields, the widow of the well-known author-publisher; Madame Blaine Bentzam, a writer for French reviews; Miss Sarah Orne Jewett, one of the most charming of New England write is, and others.

My best work in Canada was the conversion to effective voting of my good friend Robert Tyson. For years now he has done yeoman service in the cause, and has corresponded with workers all over the world on the question of electoral reform. I visited Toronto, at the invitation of Mr. William Howland, with whom I had corresponded for years. I was invited to dinner with his father, Sir William Howland, who was the first Lieutenant-Governor of Toronto after the federation of the Dominion. I found it very difficult to remember the names of the many interesting people I met there, although I could recollect the things they spoke about. Mr. Howland took me on with him to an evening garden party—quite a novel form of entertainment for me—where there were other interesting people. One of these, a lady artist who had travelled all round the world, took me on the next afternoon to an at-home at Professor Goldwin Smith's. In a talk I had with this notable man he spoke of his strong desire that Canada should become absorbed in the States; but the feeling in Canada was adverse to such a change. Still, you found Canadians everywhere, for many more men were educated than could find careers in the Dominion. Sir Sandford Fleming, the most ardent proportionalist in Canada, left Toronto on his trip to New Zealand and Australia shortly after I arrived there. I spent a few hours with him, and owed a great deal of my success in the Dominion to his influence. I felt that I had done much good in Canada, and my time was so occupied that the only thing I missed was leisure.

Much of the time in New York was spent in interviews with the various papers. I had a delightful few days at the house of Henry George, and both he and his wife did everything in their power to make my visit pleasant. Indeed, everywhere in America I received the greatest kindness and consideration. I had been 11 months in the States and Canada, and lived the strenuous life to the utmost. I had delivered over 100 lectures, travelled thousands of miles, and met the most interesting people in the world. I felt many regrets on parting with friends, comrades, sympathizers, and fellow-workers. When I reflected that on my arrival in San Francisco I knew only two persons in America in the flesh, and only two more through correspondence, and was able to look back on the hundreds of people who had personally interested me, it seemed as if there was some animal magnetism in the world, and that affinities were drawn together as if by magic.

CHAPTER XVIII
BRITAIN, THE CONTINENT, AND HOME AGAIN

I went by steamer to Glasgow, as I found the fares by that route cheaper than to Liverpool. Municipal work in that city was then attracting world-wide attention, and I enquired into the methods of taxation and the management of public works, much to my advantage. The co-operative works at Shields Hall were another source of interest to me. At Peterborough I stayed with Mr. Hare's daughter, Katie, who had married Canon Clayton. Never before did I breathe such an ecclesiastical atmosphere as in that ancient canonry, part of the old monastery, said to be 600 years old. While there I spoke to the Guild of Co-operative Women on "Australia." In Edinburgh I had a drawing-room meeting at the house of Mrs. Muir Dowie, daughter of Robert Chambers and mother of Minnie Muriel Dowie, who wrote "Through the Carpathians," and another at the Fabian Society, both on effective voting. Mrs. Dowie and Priscilla Bright McLaren, sister of John Bright, were both keen on the suffrage, and most interesting women. I had been so much associated with the suffragists in America, with the veteran Susan B. Anthony at their head, that English workers in the cause gave me a warm welcome.

London under the municipal guidance of the County Council was very different from the London I had visited 29 years earlier. Perhaps Glasgow and Birmingham have gone further in municipalizing monopolies than Londoners have, but the vastness of the scale on which London moves makes it more interesting. Cr. Peter Burt, of Glasgow, had worked hard to add publichouses to the list of things under municipal ownership and regulation, and I have always been glad to see the increasing attention paid to the Scandinavian methods of dealing with the drink traffic. I have deplored the division among temperance workers, which makes the prohibitionists hold aloof from this reform, when their aid would at least enable the experiment to be tried. But in spite of all hindrances the world moves on towards better things. It is not now a voice crying in the wilderness. There are many thousands of wise, brave, devoted men and women possessed with the enthusiasm of humanity in every civilized country, and they must prevail. Professor and Mrs. Westlake, the latter of whom was Mr. Hare's eldest daughter, arranged a most successful drawing-room meeting for me at their home, the River House, Chelsea, at which Mr. Arthur Balfour spoke. While he thought effective voting probably suitable for America and Australia, he scarcely saw the necessity for it in England. Party leaders so seldom do like to try it on themselves, but many of them are prepared to experiment on "the other fellow." In this State we find members of the Assembly anxious to try effective voting on the Legislative Council, Federal members on the State House, and vice versa. Other speakers who supported me were Sir John Lubbock (Lord Avebury), Leonard (now Lord) Courtney, Mr. Westlake, and Sir John Hall, of New Zealand. The flourishing condition of the Proportional Representation Society in England at present is due to the earnestness of the lastnamed gentlemen, and its extremely able hon. secretary (Mr. John H. Humphreys).

A few days were spent with Miss Jane Hume Clapperton, author of "Scientific Meliorism," and we had an interesting time visiting George Eliot's haunts and friends. Through the Warwickshire lanes—where the high hedges and the great trees at regular intervals made it impossible to see anything beyond, except an occasional gate, reminding me of Mrs. Browning's—

> And between the hedgerows green,
>
> How we wandered—I and you;
>
> With the bowery tops shut in,
>
> And the gates that showed the view.

—we saw the homestead known as "Mrs. Poyser's Farm," as it answers so perfectly to the description in "Adam Bede." I was taken to see Mrs. Cash, a younger friend of George Eliot, and took tea with two most interesting, old ladies—one 82, and the other 80—who had befriended the famous authoress when she was poor and stood almost alone. How I grudged the thousands of acres of beautiful agricultural land given up to shooting and hunting! We in Australia have no idea of the extent to which field sports enter into the rural life of England. People excused this love of sport to me on the ground that it is as a safety valve for the energy of idle men. Besides, said one, hunting leads, at any rate, to an appreciation of Nature; but I thought it a queer appreciation of Nature that would lead keen fox hunters to complain of the "stinking" violets that throw the hounds off the scent of the fox. I saw Ascot and Epsom, but fortunately not on a race day. A horse race I have never seen. George Moore's realistic novel "Esther Waters" does not overstate the extent to which betting demoralizes not only the wealthier, but all classes. There is a great pauper school in Sutton, where from 1,600 to 1,800 children are reared and educated. On Derby Day the children go to the side of the railroad, and catch the coppers and silver coins thrown to them by the passengers, and these are gathered together to give the children their yearly treat. But this association in the children's minds of their annual pleasure with Derby Day must, I often think, have a demoralizing tendency.

While in London I slipped in trying to avoid being run down by an omnibus and dislocated my right shoulder. I was fortunate in being the guest of Mr. and Mrs. Petherick at the time. I can never be sufficiently grateful to them for their care of and kindness to me. Only last year I went to Melbourne to meet them both again. It was the occasion of the presentation to the Federal Government of the Petherick Library, and I went over to sign and to witness the splendid deed of gift.

I have left almost to the last of the account of my English visit all mention of the Baconians I met and from whom I gained valuable information in corroboration of the Baconian authorship. In some circles I found that, to suggest that Shakspeare did not write the plays and poems was equal to throwing a bombshell among them. As a Baconian I received an invitation to a picnic at the beautiful country house of Mr. Edwin Lawrence, with whom I had a pleasant talk. The house was built on a part of a royal forest, in which firs and pines were planted at the time of the great Napoleonic wars when timber could not be got from the Baltic and England had to trust to her own hearts of oak and her own growth of pine for masts and planks. Mr. Lawrence had written pamphlets and essays on the Baconian theory, and I found my knowledge of the subject expanding and growing under his intelligent talk. His wife's father (J. Benjamin Smith) had taught Cobden the ethics of free trade. It was through the kind liberality of Miss Florence Davenport Hill that a pamphlet, recording the speeches and results of the voting at River House, Chelsea, was printed and circulated. When I visited Miss Hill and her sister and found them as eager for social and political reform as they had been 29 years earlier, I had another proof of the eternal youth which large and high interests keep within us in spite of advancing years. Miss Davenport Hill had been a member of the London School Board for 15 years, and was reelected after I left England. Years of her life had been devoted to work for the children of the State, and she was a member of the Board of Guardians for the populous union of St. Pancras. Everyone acknowledged the great good that the admission of women to those boards had done. I spent a pleasant time at Toynbee Hall, a University centre, in the poorest part of London, founded by men. Canon and Mrs. Barrett were intensely interested in South Australian work for State children. Similar University centres which I visited in America, like Hull House, in Chicago, were founded by women graduates. Mrs. Fawcett I met several times, but Mrs. Garrett Anderson only once. When the suffrage was granted to the women of South Australia I received a letter of congratulation from Dr. Helen Blackburn, one of the first women to take a medical degree. Nowadays women doctors are accepted as part of our daily life, and it is to these brave pioneers of the women's cause, Drs. Elizabeth Blackwell, Helen Rackburn, Garrett Anderson, and other like noble souls, that the social and political prestige of women has advanced so tremendously all over the English-speaking world. It only remains now for a few women, full of the enthusiasm of humanity and gifted with the power of public speaking, to gain another and important step for the womanhood of the world in the direction of economic freedom. Before leaving England I was gratified at receiving a cheque from Mrs. Westlake, contributed by the English proportionalists, to help me in the cause. This was the second gift of the kind I had received, for my friends in San Francisco had already helped me financially on my way to reform. Socially I liked the atmosphere of America better than that of England, but politically England was infinitely more advanced. Steadily and surely a safer democracy seems to be evolving in the old country than in the Transatlantic Republic. I left England at the end of September, 1894.

My intended visit to Paris was cancelled through the death a short time before of the only friend I wished to meet there, the Baroness Blaze-de-Bury, and I went straight through to Bale. I made a detour to Zurich, where I hoped to see people interested in proportional representation who could speak English. An interesting fellow-worker in the cause was Herr Karl Burkli, to whom I suggested the idea of lecturing with ballots. The oldest advocate of proportional representation on the Continent, M. Ernest Naville, I met at Geneva. In that tiny republic in the heart of Europe, which is the home of experimental legislation, I found effective voting already established in four cantons, and the effect in these cantons had been so good (said Ernest Naville) "that it is only a matter of time to see all the Swiss cantons and the Swiss Federation adopt it." In Zurich Herr Burkli was delighted that they had introduced progressive taxation into the canton, but the effect had been to drive away the wealthy people who came in search of quiet and healthy residence. Progressive taxation has not by any means proved the unmixed blessing which so many of its advocates claim it to be. In New Zealand, we are told, on the best authority, that land monopoly and land jobbery were never so rampant in the Dominion as since the introduction of the progressive land tax. One wondered how the three million Swiss people lived on their little territory, so much occupied by barren mountain, and lakes which supply only a few fish. My Zurich friends told me that it was by their unremitting industry and exceptional thrift, but others said that the foreign visitors who go to the recreation ground of Europe circulate so much money that instead of the prayer "Give us this day our daily bread" the Swiss people ask, "Send us this day one foreigner."

In Italy I saw the most intense culture in the world—no pleasure grounds or deer parks for the wealthy. The whole country looked like a garden with trellised vines and laden trees. Italian wine was grown, principally for home consumption, and that was immense. Prohibitionists would speak to deaf ears there. Wine was not a luxury, but a necessity of life. It made the poor fare of dry bread and polenta (maize porridge) go down more pleasantly. It was the greater abundance of fruit and wine that caused the Italian poorer classes to look healthier than the German. In Germany, which taxed itself to give cheap beet sugar to the British consumer, the people paid 6d. a lb. for the little they could afford to use; and in Italy it was nearly 8d.—a source of revenue to the Governments, but prohibitive to the poor. There were no sweet shops in Italy. England only could afford such luxuries. I visited at Siena a home for deaf mutes, and found that each child had wine at two of its daily meals—about a pint a day. It was the light-red wine of the country, with little alcohol in it; but those who warn us against looking on the wine when it is red will be shocked to hear of these little ones drinking it like milk. Those, however, who live in Italy say that not once a year do they see any one drunk in the streets.

I reached South Australia on December 12, 1894, after an absence of 20 months. I found the women's suffrage movement wavering in the balance. It had apparently come with a rush—as unexpected as it was welcome to those whose strenuous exertions at last seemed likely to be crowned with success. Though sympathetic to the cause, I had always been regarded as a weakkneed sister by the real workers. I had failed to see the advantage of having a vote that might leave me after an election a disfranchised voter, instead of an unenfranchised woman. People talk of citizens being disfranchised for the Legislative Council when they really mean that they are unenfranchised. You can scarcely be disfranchised if you have never been enfranchised; and I have regarded the enfranchisement of the people on the roll as more important for the time being than adding new names to the rolls. This would only tend to increase the disproportion between the representative and the represented. But I rejoiced when the Women's Suffrage Bill was carried, for I believe that women have thought more and accepted the responsibilities of voting to a greater extent than was ever expected of them. During the week I was accorded a welcome home in the old Academy of Music, Rundle street, where I listened with embarrassment to the avalanche of eulogium that overwhelmed me. "What a good thing it is, Miss Spence, that you have only one idea," a gentleman once said to me on my country tour. He wished thus to express his feeling concerning my singleness of purpose towards effective voting. But at this welcome home I felt that others realized what I had often said myself. It is really because I have so many ideas for making life better, wiser, and pleasanter all of which effective voting will aid—that I seem so absorbed in the one reform. My opinions on other matters I give for what they are worth—for discussion, for acceptance or rejection. My opinions on equitable representation I hold absolutely, subject to criticism of methods but impregnable as to principle.

CHAPTER XIX
PROGRESS OF EFFECTIVE VOTING

My journalistic work after my return was neither so regular nor so profitable as before I left Adelaide. The bank failures had affected me rather badly, and financially my outlook was anything but rosy in the year 1895. There was, however, plenty of public work open to me, and, in addition to the many lectures I gave in various parts of the State on effective voting, I became a member of the Hospital Commission, appointed that year by the Kingston Government to enquire into the trouble at the Adelaide Hospital. That same year saw a decided step taken in connection with effective voting, and in July a league was formed, which has been in existence ever since. I was appointed the first President, my brother John became secretary pro tem, and Mr. A. W. Piper the first treasurer. I felt at last that the reform was taking definite shape, and looked hopefully to its future. The following year was especially interesting to the women of South Australia, and, indeed, to suffragists all over the world, for at the general election of 1896 women, for the first time in Australia, had the right to vote. New Zealand had preceded us with this reform, but the first election in this State found many women voters fairly well equipped to accept their responsibilities as citizens of the State. But in the full realization by the majority of women of their whole duties of citizenship I have been distinctly disappointed. Not that they have been on the whole less patriotic and less zealous than men voters; but, like their brothers, they have allowed their interest in public affairs to stop short at the act of voting, as if the right to vote were the beginning and the end of political life. There has been too great a tendency on the part of women to allow reform work—particularly women's branches of it—to be done by a few disinterested and public-spirited women. Not only is the home the centre of woman's sphere, as it should be, but in too many cases it is permitted to be its limitation. The larger social life has been ignored, and women have consequently failed to have the effect on public life of which their political privilege is capable.

At the close of a second lecturing tour through the State, during which I visited and spoke at most of the village settlements, I received an invitation from the Women's Land Reform League to attend a social gathering at the residence of Miss Sutherland, Clark street, Norwood. The occasion was my seventy-first birthday, and my friends had chosen that day (October 31, 1896) to mark their appreciation of my public services. There were about 30 of the members present, all interesting by reason of their zealous care for the welfare of the State. Their President (Mrs. C. Proud) presented me, on behalf of the members, with a lady's handbag, ornamented with a silver plate, bearing my name, the date of the presentation, and the name of the cause for which I stood. From that day the little bag has been the inseparable companion of all my wanderings, and a constant reminder of the many kind friends who, with me, had realized that "love of country is one of the loftiest virtues which the Almighty has planted in the human heart." That association was the first in South Australia to place effective voting on its platform.

My long comradeship with Mrs. A. H. Young began before the close of the year. A disfranchised voter at her first election, she was driven farther afield than the present inadequate system of voting to look for a just electoral method. She found it in effective voting, and from that time devoted herself to the cause. Early in 1897 Mrs. Young was appointed the first honorary secretary of the league. January of the same year found us stirred to action by the success of Sir Edward Braddon's first Bill for proportional representation in Tasmania. Though limited in its application to the two chief cities of the island State, the experiment was wholly successful. We had our first large public meeting in the Co-operative Hall in January, and carried a resolution protesting against the use of the block vote for the Federal Convention elections. A deputation to the acting Premier (Mr.—afterwards Sir Frederick—Holder) was arranged for the next morning. But we were disappointed in the result of our mission, for Mr. Holder pointed out that the Enabling Act distinctly provided for every elector having 10 votes, and effective voting meant a single transferable vote. I had written and telegraphed to the Hon. C. C. Kingston when the Enabling Act was being drafted to beg him to consider effective voting as the basis of election; but he did not see it then, nor did he ever see it. In spite, however, of the short sightedness of party leaders, events began to move quickly.

Our disappointment over the maintenance of the block vote for the election of 10 delegates to the Federal Convention led to my brother John's suggestion that I should become a candidate. Startling as the suggestion was, so many of my friends supported it that I agreed to do so. I maintained that the fundamental necessity of a democratic Constitution such as we hoped would evolve from the combined efforts of the ablest men in the Australian States was a just system of representation and it was as the advocate of effective voting that I took my stand. My personal observation in the United States and Canada had impressed me with the dangers inseparable from the election of Federal Legislatures by local majorities—sometimes by minorities—where money and influence could be employed, particularly where a line in a tariff spelt a fortune to a section of the people, in the manipulation of the floating vote. Parties may boast of their voting strength and their compactness, but their voting strength under the present system of voting is only as strong as its weakest link, discordant or discontented minorities, will permit it to be. The stronger a party is in the Legislature the more is expected from it by every little section of voters to whom it owes its victory at the polls. The impelling force of responsibility which makes all Governments "go slow" creates the greatest discontent among impatient followers of the rank and file, and where a few votes may turn the scale at any general election a Government is often compelled to choose between yielding to the demands of its more clamorous followers at the expense of the general taxpayer or submitting to a Ministerial defeat.

As much as we may talk of democracy in Australia, we are far from realizing a truly democratic ideal. A State in a pure democracy draws no nice and invidious distinctions between man and man. She disclaims the right of favouring either property, education, talent, or virtue. She conceives that all alike have an interest in good government, and that all who form the community, of full age and untainted by crime, should have a right to their share in the representation. She allows education to exert its legitimate power through the press; talent in every department of business, property in its social and material advantages; virtue and religion to influence public opinion and the public conscience. But she views all men as politically equal, and rightly so, if the equality is to be as real in operation as in theory. If the equality is actual in the representation of the citizens—truth and virtue, being stronger than error and vice, and wisdom being greater than folly, when a fair field is offered—the higher qualities subdue the lower and make themselves felt in every department of the State. But if the representation from defective machinery is not equal, the balance is overthrown, and neither education, talent, nor virtue can work through public opinion so as to have any beneficial influence on politics. We know that in despotisms and oligarchies, where the majority are unrepresented and the few extinguish the many, independence of thought is crushed down, talent is bribed to do service to tyranny, education is confined to a privileged class and denied to the people, property is sometimes pillaged and sometimes flattered, and even virtue is degraded by lowering its field and making subservience appear to be patience and loyalty, and religion is not unfrequently made the handmaid of oppression. Taxes fall heavily on the poor for the benefit of the rich, and the only check proceeds from the fear of rebellion. When, on the other hand, the majority extinguishes the minority, the evil effects are not so apparent. The body oppressed is smaller and generally wealthier, with many social advantages to draw off attention from the political injustice under which they suffer; but there is the same want of sympathy between class and class, moral courage is rare, talent is perverted, genius is overlooked, education is general, but superficial, and press and Pulpit often timid in exposing or denouncing popular errors. An average standard of virtue is all that is aimed at, and when no higher mark is set up there is great fear of falling below the average. Therefore it is incumbent on all States to look well to it that their representative systems really secure the political equality they all profess to give, for until that is done democracy has had no fair trial.

In framing a new constitution the opportunity arose for laying the foundation of just representation, and, had I been elected, my first and last thought would have been given to the claims of the whole people to electoral justice. But the 7,500 votes which I received left me far enough from the lucky 10. Had Mr. Kingston not asserted both publicly and privately that, if elected, I could not constitutionally take my seat, I might have done better. There were rumours even that my nomination paper would be rejected. But to obviate this, Mrs. Young, who got it filled in, was careful to see that no name was on it that had no right there, and its presentation was delayed till five minutes before the hour of noon, in order that no time would be left to upset its validity. From a press cutting on the declaration of the poll I cull this item of news—"Several unexpected candidates were announced, but the only nomination which evoked any expressions of approval was that of Miss Spence." I was the first woman in Australia to seek election in a political contest. From the two main party lists I was, of course, excluded, but in the list of the "10 best men" selected by a Liberal organization my name appeared. When the list was taken to the printer—who, I think, happened to be the late Federal member, Mr. James Hutchison—he objected to the heading of the "10 best men," as one of them was a woman. He suggested that my name should be dropped, and a man's put in its place. "You can't say Miss Spence is one of the '10 best men.' Take her name out." "Not say she's one of the '10 best men?'" the Liberal organizer objected, "Why she's the best man of the lot." I had not expected to be elected, but I did expect that my candidature would help effective voting, and I am sure it did. Later the league arranged a deputation to Mr. Kingston, to beg him to use his influence for the adoption of the principle in time for the first Federal elections. We foresaw, and prophesied what has actually occurred—the monopoly of representation by one party in the Senate, and the consequent disfranchisement of hundreds of thousands of voters throughout the Commonwealth. But, as before, Mr. Kingston declined to see the writing on the wall. The Hon. D. M. Charleston was successful in carrying through the Legislative Council a motion in favour of its application to Federal elections, but Mr. Wynn in the Lower House had a harder row to hoe, and a division was never taken.

Mrs. Young and I spent a pleasant evening at Government House in July of the same year, as Sir Fowell and Lady Buxton had expressed a desire to understand the system. In addition to a large house party, several prominent citizens were present, and all were greatly interested. On leaving at 11 o'clock we found the gate closed against us, as the porter was evidently unaware that visitors were being entertained. We were amused at the indignation of the London-bred butler, who, on coming to our rescue, cried with a perfect Cockney accent, "Gyte, gyte, yer don't lock gytes till visitors is off." This was a memorable year in the annals of our cause, for on his election to fill an extraordinary vacancy for North Adelaide Mr. Glynn promised to introduce effective voting into the House. This he did in July by tabling a motion for the adoption of the principle, and we were pleased to find in Mr. Batchelor, now the Minister for External Affairs in the Federal Government, a stanch supporter. Among the many politicians who have blown hot and cold on the reform as occasion arose, Mr. Batchelor has steadily and consistently remained a supporter of what he terms "the only system that makes majority rule possible."

When Mrs. Young and I began our work together the question was frequently asked why women alone were working for effective voting? The answer was simple. There were few men with leisure in South Australia, and, if there were, the leisured man was scarcely likely to take up reform work. When I first seized hold of this reform women as platform speakers were unheard of. Indeed, the prejudice was so strong against women in public life that although I wrote the letters to The Melbourne Argus it was my brother John who was nominally the correspondent. So for 30 years I wrote anonymously to the press on this subject. I waited for some man to come forward and do the platform work for me. We women are accused of waiting and waiting for the coming man, but often he doesn't come at all; and oftener still, when he does come, we should be a great deal better without him. In this case he did not come at all, and I started to do the work myself; and, just because I was a woman working singlehanded in the cause, Mrs. Young joined me in the crusade against inequitable representation. For many years, however, the cause has counted to its credit men speakers and demonstrators of ability and talent all over the State, who are carrying the gospel of representative reform into every camp, both friendly and hostile.

It was said of Gibbon when his autobiography was published that he did not know the difference between himself and the Roman Empire. I have sometimes thought that the same charge might be levelled against me with regard to effective voting; but association with a reform for half a century sometimes makes it difficult to separate the interests of the person from the interests of the cause. Following on my return from America effective voting played a larger part than ever in my life. I had come back cheered by the earnestness and enthusiasm of American reformers, and I found the people of my adopted country more than ever prepared to listen to my teaching. Parties had become more clearly defined, and the results of our system of education were beginning to tell, I think, in the increased interest taken by individuals as well as by societies in social and economic questions. I found interesting people everywhere, in every mode of life, and in every class of society. My friends sometimes accused me of judging people's intelligence by the interest they took in effective voting; but, although this may have been true to a certain extent, it was not wholly correct. Certainly I felt more drawn to effective voters, but there are friendships I value highly into which my special reform work never enters. Just as the more recent years of my life have been coloured by the growth of the movement which means more to me than anything else in the world, so must the remaining chapters of this narrative bear the imprint of its influence.

CHAPTER XX
WIDENING INTERESTS

During this period my work on the State Children's Council continued, and I never found time hang heavily on my hands; so that when Mr. Kingston met me one day later in the year, and told me he particularly wished me to accept an appointment as a member of the Destitute Board, I hesitated. "I am too old," I objected. "No, no, Miss Spence," he replied laughingly, "it is only we who grow old—you have the gift of perpetual youth." But I was nearly 72, and at any rate I thought I should first consult my friends. I found them all eager that I should accept the position. I had agitated long and often for the appointment of women on all public boards, particularly where both sexes came under treatment, and I accepted the post. Although often I have found the work tiring, I have never regretted the step I took in joining the board. Experience has emphasized my early desire that two women at least should occupy positions on it. I hope that future Governments will rectify the mistake of past years by utilizing to a greater extent the valuable aid of capable and sympathetic women in a branch of public work for which they are peculiarly fitted. Early in my career as a member of the board I found grave defects in the daily bill of fare, and set myself to the task of remedying them as far as lay in my power. For 30 years the same kind of soup, day in and day out, followed by the eternal and evergreen cabbage as a vegetable, in season and out of season, found its way to the table. My own tastes and mode of life were simplicity personified, but my stomach revolted against a dietary as unvaried as it was unappetizing. An old servant who heard that I attended the Destitute Asylum every week was loud in her lamentations that "poor dear Miss Spence was so reduced that she had to go to the Destitute every week for rations!" My thankfulness that she had misconceived the position stirred me to leave no stone unturned for the betterment of the destitute bill of fare. I was successful, and the varied diet now enjoyed bears witness to the humanitarian views of all the members of the board, who were as anxious to help in the reform as I was. My heart has always gone out to the poor old folk whose faces bear the impress of long years of strenuous toil and who at the close of life at least should find a haven of restfulness and peace in the State for whose advancement they have laboured in the past.

She was a witty woman who divided autobiographies into two classes... autobiographies and ought-not-to-biographies—but I am sure she never attempted to write one herself. There is so much in one's life that looms large from a personal point of view about which other people would care little, and the difficulty often arises, not so much about what to put in as what to leave out.

How much my personal interests had widened during my absence from home could be gauged somewhat by the enormous increase in my correspondence after my return. American, Canadian, English, and Continental correspondents have kept me for many years well informed on reform and kindred subjects; and the letters I have received, and the replies they have drawn from me, go far to make me doubt the accuracy of the accepted belief that "letter writing has become a lost art." A full mind with a facile pen makes letter writing a joy, and both of these attributes I think I may fairly claim. My correspondence with Alfred Cridge was kept up till his death a few years ago, and his son, following worthily in the footsteps of a noble father, has taken up the broken threads of the lifework of my friend, and is doing his utmost to carry it to a successful issue. My love of reading, which has been a characteristic feature of my life, found full scope for expression in the piles of books which reached us from all parts of the world. It has always been my desire to keep abreast of current literature, and this, by means of my book club and other sources, I was able to do. Sometimes my friends from abroad sent me copies of their own publications, Dr. Bayard Holmes invariably forwarding to me a presentation copy of his most valuable treatises on medical subjects. Mrs. Stetson's poems and economic writings have always proved a source of inspiration to me, and I have distributed her books wherever I have thought they would be appreciated. Just at this time my financial position became brighter. I was fortunate in being able to dispose of my two properties in East Adelaide, and the purchasing of an annuity freed me entirely from money and domestic worries. Perhaps the greatest joy of all was that I was once more able to follow my charitable inclinations by giving that little mite which, coming opportunely, gladdens the heart of the disconsolate widow or smoothes the path of the struggling worker. Giving up my home entirely, I went to live with my dear friend Mrs. Baker, at Osmond terrace, where, perhaps, I spent the most restful period of a somewhat eventful life.

The inauguration of a Criminological Society in Adelaide was a welcome sign to me of the growing public interest in methods of prison discipline and treatment. I was one of the foundation members of the society, and attended every meeting during its short existence. My one contribution to the lectures delivered under its auspices was on "Heredity and Environment." This was a subject in which I had long been interested, holding the view that environment had more to do with the building up of character than heredity had to do with its decadence. How much or how little truth there is in the cynical observation that the only believers in heredity nowadays are the fathers of very clever sons I am not prepared to say. I do say, however, that with the cruel and hopeless law of heredity as laid down by Zola and Ibsen I have little sympathy. According to these pessimists, who ride heredity to death, we inherit only the vices, the weaknesses, and the diseases of our ancestors. If this, however, were really the case, the world would be growing worse and not better, as it assuredly is, with every succeeding generation. The contrary view taken of the matter by Ibsen's fellowcountryman, Bjornsen, appears to me to be so much more commonsense and humanizing. He holds that if we know that our ancestors drank and gambled to excess, or were violent-tempered or immoral, we can quite easily avoid the pitfall, knowing it to be there. Too readily wrongdoers are prepared to lay their failings at the door of ancestors, society, or some other blamable source, instead of attributing them, as they should do, to their own selfish and weak indulgence and lack of self-control. Heredity, though an enormous factor in our constitution, need not be regarded as an over-mastering fate, for each human being has an almost limitless parentage to draw upon.

Each child has both a father and a mother, and two grandparents on both sides, increasing as one goes back. But, besides drawing on a much wider ancestry than the immediate parents, we have more than we inherit, or where could the law of progress operate? Each generation, each child who is born, comes into a slightly different world, fed by more experience, blown upon by fresh influences. And each individual comes into the world, not with a body merely, but with a soul; and this soul is susceptible to impressions, not only from the outer material world but from the other souls also impressed by the old and the new, by the material and the ideal.

"The History of the Jukes" is continually cited as proving the power and force of heredity. Most people who read the book through, however, instead of merely accepting allusions one-sided and defective to it, see clearly that it forms the strongest argument for change of environment that ever was brought forward. The assumed name of Jukes is given to the descendants of a worthless woman who emigrated to America upwards of a century and a half ago, and from whom hundreds of criminals, paupers, and prostitutes have descended. But how were the Jukes' descendants dealt with during this period? No helping hand removed the children from their vicious and criminal surroundings known as one of the crime-cradles of the State of New York. Neither church nor school took them under its protecting care. Born and reared in the haunts of vice and crime, nothing but viciousness and criminality could be expected as a result. Without going, so far as a wellknown ex-member of our State Legislature, whose antagonism to the humanitarian treatment of prisoners led him to the belief that "there wasn't nothin' in 'erry-ditty,' it was all tommy rot," I still hold to the belief that environment plays the larger part in the formation of character. Every phase of criminal reform is, I candidly admit, dealing with effects rather than causes. Effects, however, must be dealt with, and the more humanely they are dealt with the better for society at large. So long as society shuts its eyes to the social conditions under which the masses of the people live, move, and have their being as tending towards lowering rather than uplifting the individual and the community, the supply of cases for criminal treatment will unfortunately show little tendency to decrease. The work before reformers of the world is to prevent the creation of criminals by changing the environment of those with criminal tendencies as well as to seek to alleviate the resulting disease by methods of criminal reform.

Many interesting lectures were given by prominent citizens under the auspices of the society, which did a great deal to awaken the public conscience on the important question of criminal reform. The Rev. J. Day Thompson, who was then in the zenith of his intellectual power and a noble supporter of all things that tended to the uplifting of humanity, dealt with the land question in relation to crime. He gave a telling illustration of his point—which I thought equally applicable to the question of environment in relation to prison reform—that no permanent good could result from social legislation until society recognised and dealt with the root of the social evil, the land question. "In a lunatic asylum," he said, "it is the custom to test the sanity of patients by giving them a ladle with which to empty a tub of water standing under a running tap. 'How do you decide?' the warder was asked. 'Why, them as isn't idiots stops the tap.'" It was the Rev. J. Day Thompson who first called me the "Grand Old Woman" of South Australia. When he left Adelaide for the wider sphere of service open to him in England I felt that we had lost one of the most cultured and able men who had ever come among us, and one whom no community could lose without being distinctly the poorer for his absence.

Just at this time the visit of Dr. and Mrs. Mills created a little excitement in certain circles. Their lectures on Christian science, both public and private, were wonderfully well attended, and I missed few of them. I have all my life endeavoured to keep an open mind on these questions, and have been prepared to accept new ideas and new modes of thought. But, although I found much that was charming in the lectures that swayed the minds of so many of my friends, I found little to convince me that Christian scientists were right and the rest of the world wrong in their interpretation of the meaning of life. So far as the cultivation of will power, as it is called, is concerned, I have no quarrel with those who maintain that a power of self-control is the basis of human happiness. So far as the will can be trained to obey only those instincts that tend to the growth and maintenance of self-respect—to prevent the subordination of our better feelings to the overpowering effects of passion, greed, or injustice—it must help to the development of one of the primary necessities of a sane existence. When, however, the same agency is brought to bear on the treatment of diseases in any shape or form I find my faith wavering. Though there may be more things in earth and heaven than are dreamed of in my philosophy, I was not prepared to follow the teachings set before us by the interpreters of this belief, whose visit had made an interesting break in the lives of many people. Truth I find everywhere expressed, goodness in all things; but I neither look for nor expect perfection in any one thing the world has ever produced. "Tell me where God is," a somewhat, cynical sceptic asked of a child. "Tell me where He is not," replied the child; and the same thing applies to goodness. Do not tell me where goodness is, but point out to, me, if you can, where it is not. It is for each one to find out for himself where the right path lies, and to follow it with all his strength of mind and of purpose. Pippa's song, "God's in His heaven-all's right with the world," does not mean that the time has come for us to lay down our arms in the battle of right against wrong. No! no; it is an inspiration for us to gird our loins afresh, to "right the wrongs that need resistance;" for, God being in His heaven, and the world itself being right, makes it so much easier to correct mistakes that are due to human agencies and shortcomings only.

I found time to spend a pleasant week at Victor Harbour with my friends, Mr. and Mrs. John Wyles. I remember one day being asked whether I was not sorry I never married. "No," I replied, "for, although I often envy my friends the happiness they find in their children, I have never envied them their husbands." I think we must have been in a frivolous mood; for a lady visitor, who was present, capped my remark with the statement that she was quite sure Miss Spence was thankful that when she died she would not be described as the "relic" of any man. It was the same lady who on another occasion, when one of the juvenile members of the party asked whether poets had to pay for poetical licence, wittily replied, "No, my dear, but their readers do!" Although so much of my time has been spent in public work, I have by no means neglected or despised the social side of life. Visits to my friends have always been delightful to me, and I have felt as much interested in the domestic virtues of my many acquaintances as I have been an admirer of their grasp of literature, politics, or any branch of the arts or sciences in which they have been interested. This seaside visit had been a welcome break in a year that had brought me a new occupation as a member of the Destitute Board, had given me the experience of a political campaign, had witnessed the framing of the Constitution for the Commonwealth 'neath the Southern Cross, and had seen effective voting advance from the academic stage into the realm of practical politics. During the year Mrs. Young and I addressed together 26 meetings on this subject. One of the most interesting was at the Blind School, North Adelaide. The keenness with which this audience gripped every detail of the explanation showed us how splendidly they had risen above their affliction. I was reminded of Helen Keller, the American girl, who at the age of 21 months had lost sight and hearing, and whom I had met in Chicago during my American visit, just before she took her degree at Harvard University.

To all peacelovers the years from 1898 to 1901 were shadowed by the South African war. The din of battle was in our ears only to a less degree than in those of our kinsmen in the mother country. War has always been abhorrent to me, and there was the additional objection to my mind in the case of the South African war in that it was altogether unjustified. Froude's chapters on South Africa had impressed me on the publication of his book "Oceana," after his visit here in the seventies. His indictment of England for her treatment of the Boers from the earliest days of her occupation of Cape Colony was too powerful to be ignored. I felt it to be impossible that so great a historian as Froude should make such grave charges on insufficient evidence. The annexation of 1877, so bitterly condemned by him, followed by the treaty of peace of 1881, with its famous "suzerainty" clause, was, I think, but a stepping stone to the war which was said to have embittered the last years of the life of Queen Victoria. The one voice raised in protest against the annexation of 1877 in the British House of

Commons was that of Mr. Leonard (now Lord) Courtney. Not afraid to stand alone, though all the world were against him, the war at the close of the century found Leonard Courtney again taking his stand against the majority of his countrymen, and this time it cost him his Parliamentary seat. I have often felt proud that the leadership of proportional representation in England should have fallen into the hands of so morally courageous a man as Leonard Courtney has invariably proved himself to be.

We are apt to pride ourselves on the advance we have made in our civilization; but our self-glorification received a rude shock at the feelings of intolerance and race hatred that the war brought forth. Freedom of speech became the monopoly of those who supported the war, and the person who dared to express an opinion which differed from that of the majority needed a great deal more than the ordinary allowance of moral courage. Unfortunately the intolerance so characteristic of that period is a feature, to a greater or lesser extent, of every Parliamentary election in the Commonwealth. The clause in the Federal Electoral Act which makes disturbance of a political meeting a penal offence is a curious reflection on a so-called democratic community. But, though its justification can scarcely be denied even by the partisans of the noisier elements in a political crowd, its existence must be deplored by every right-minded and truehearted citizen. In Miss Rose Scott I found a sympathizer on this question of the war; and one of the best speeches I ever heard her make was on Peace and Arbitration. "Mafeking Day" was celebrated while we were in Sydney, and I remember how we three—Miss Scott, Mrs. Young, and I—remained indoors the whole day, at the charming home of our hostess, on Point Piper road. The black band of death and desolation was too apparent for us to feel that we could face the almost ribald excesses of that day. I felt the war far less keenly than did my two friends; but it was bad even for me. No one called, and the only companions of our chosen solitude were the books we all loved so much, and

> The secret sympathy,
>
> The silver link, the silken tie,

Which heart to heart and mind to mind,

In body and in soul can bind.

I had hoped that the Women's National Council, a branch of which was formed in Adelaide a few years later, would have made a great deal of the question of peace and arbitration, just as other branches have done all over the world; and when the Peace Society was inaugurated a short time ago I was glad to be able to express my sympathy with the movement by becoming a member. As I was returning from a lecturing tour in the south during this time, an old Scotch farm-wife came into the carriage where I had been knitting in solitude. She was a woman of strong feelings, and was bitterly opposed to the war. We chatted on the subject for a time, getting along famously, until she discovered that I was Miss Spence. "But you are a Unitarian!" she protested in a shocked tone. I admitted the fact. "Oh, Miss Spence," she went on, "how can you be so wicked as to deny the divinity of Christ?" I explained to her what Unitarianism was, but she held dubiously aloof for a time. Then we talked of other things. She told me of many family affairs, and when she left me at the station she said, "All, well, Miss Spence, I've learned something this morning, and that is that a Unitarian can be just as good and honest as other folk."

CHAPTER XXI
PROPORTIONAL REPRESENTATION AND FEDERATION

In the debates of the Federal Convention I was naturally much interested. Many times I regretted my failure to win a seat when I saw how, in spite of warnings against, and years of lamentable experience of, a vicious system of voting, the members of the Convention went calmly on their way, accepting as a matter of course the crude and haphazard methods known to them, the unscientific system of voting so dear to the heart of the "middling" politician and the party intriguer. I believe Mr. Glynn alone raised his voice in favour of proportional representation, in the Convention, as he has done consistently in every representative assembly of which he has been a member. Instead of seeing to it that the foundations of the Commonwealth were "broad based upon the people's will" by the adoption of effective voting, and thus maintaining the necessary connection between the representative and the represented, these thinkers for the people at the very outset of federation sowed the seeds of future discontent and Federal apathy. Faced with disfranchisement for three or six years, possibly for ever—so long as the present system of voting remains—it is unreasonable to expect from the people as a whole that interest in the national well-being which alone can lead to the safety of a progressive nation.

Proportional representation was for long talked of as a device for representing minorities. It is only in recent years that the real scope of the reform has been recognised. By no other means than the adoption of the single transferable vote can the rule of the majority obtain. The fundamental principle of proportional representation is that majorities must rule, but that minorities shall be adequately represented. An intelligent minority of representatives has great weight and influence. Its voice can be heard. It can fully and truly express the views of the voters it represents. It can watch the majority and keep it straight. These clear rights of the minority are denied by the use of the multiple vote. It has also been asked—Can a Government be as strong as it needs to be when—besides the organized Ministerial party and the recognised Opposition—there may be a larger number of independent members than at present who may vote either way? It is quite possible for a Government to be too strong, and this is especially dangerous in Australia, where there are so many of what are known as optional functions of government undertaken and administered by the Ministry of the day, resting on a majority in the Legislature. To maintain this ascendancy concessions are made to the personal interests of members or to local or class interests of their constituencies at the cost of the whole country.

When introducing proportional representation into the Belgian Chamber the Prime Minister (M. Bernhaert) spoke well and forcibly on the subject of a strong Government:—

I, who have the honour of speaking to you to-day in the name of the Government and who have at my back the strongest majority that was ever known in Belgium, owe it to truth to say that our opinions have not a corresponding preponderance in the country; and I believe that, if that majority were always correctly expressed, we should gain in stability what we might lose in apparent strength. Gentlemen, in the actual state of things, to whom belongs the Government of the country? It belongs to some two or three thousand electors, who assuredly are neither the best nor the most intelligent, who turn the scale at each of our scrutin de liste elections. I see to the right and to the left two large armies—Catholics and Liberals—of force almost equal, whom nothing would tempt to desert their standard, who serve it with devotion and from conviction. Well, these great armies do not count, or scarcely count. On the day of battle it is as if they do not exist. What counts, what decides, what triumphs, is another body of electors altogether—a floating body too often swayed by their passions, by their prejudices; or, worse still, by their interests. These are our masters, and according as they veer from right to left, or from left to right, the Government of the country changes, and its history takes a new direction. Gentlemen, is it well that it should be so? Is it well that this country should be at the mercy of such contemptible elements as these?

How often have I longed to see a Premier in this, my adopted country, rise to such fervid heights of patriotism as this?

M. Bernhaert is right. It is the party Government that is essentially the weak Government. It cannot afford to estrange or offend any one who commands votes. It is said that every prominent politician in the British House of Commons is being perpetually tempted and tormented by his friends not to be honest, and perpetually assailed by his enemies in order to be made to appear to be dishonest. The Opposition is prepared to trip up the Ministry at every step. It exaggerates mistakes, misrepresents motives, and combats measures which it believes to be good, if these are brought forward by its opponents. It bullies in public and undermines in secret. It is always ready to step into the shoes of the Ministry, to undergo similar treatment. This is the sort of strength which is supposed to be imperilled if the nation were equitably represented in the Legislature. In the present state of the world, especially in the Australian States, where the functions of government have multiplied and are multiplying, it is of the first importance that the administration should be watched from all sides, and not merely from the point of view of those who wish to sit on the Treasury benches. The right function of the Opposition is to see that the Government does the work of the country well. The actual practice of the Opposition is to try to prevent it from doing the country's work at all. In order that government should be honest, intelligent, and economical, it needs helpful criticism rather than unqualified opposition; and this criticism may be expected from the less compact and more independent ranks in a legislative body which truly represents all the people. Party discipline, which is almost inevitable in the present struggle for ascendancy or defeat, is the most undemocratic agency in the world. It is rather by liberating all votes and allowing them to group themselves according to conviction that a real government of the people by the people can be secured. When I look back on the intention of the framers of the Commonwealth Constitution to create in the Senate a States' rights House I am amazed at the remoteness of the intention from the achievement. The Senate is as much a party House as is the House of Representatives. Nothing, perhaps, describes the position better than the epigrammatic if somewhat triumphant statement of a Labour Senator some time ago. "The Senate was supposed to be a place where the radical legislation of the Lower Chamber could be cooled off, but they had found that the saucer was hotter than the cup."

The long illness and death of my ward, Mrs. Hood, once more gave to my life a new direction. History was repeating itself. Just as 40 years earlier Mrs. Hood and her brothers had been left in my charge on the death of their mother, so once again a dying mother begged me to accept the guardianship of her three orphan children. Verging as they were on the threshold of manhood and womanhood, they scarcely needed the care and attention due to smaller children, but I realized I think to the full, what so many parents have realized—that the responsibilities for the training of children of an older growth are greater and more burdensome than the physical care of the infant. The family belongings were gathered in from the four quarters of the globe to which they had been scattered on my giving up housekeeping, and we again began a family life in Kent Town. Soon after we had settled, the motion in charge of the Hon. D. M. Charleston in favour of the adoption of proportional representation for Federal elections was carried to a successful issue in the Legislative Council. The Hon. A. A. Kirkpatrick suggested the advisableness of preparing a Bill at this stage. A motion simply affirming a principle, he said, was not likely to carry the cause much further, as it left the question of the application of the principle too much an open one. The league, he thought, should have something definite to put before candidates, so that a definite answer could be obtained from them. In New Zealand, Mr. O'Regan, a well-known solicitor, had also introduced into the House of Representatives during 1898 a Bill for the adoption of effective voting. Unfortunately members had become wedded to single electorates, and when a change was made it was to second ballots—a system of voting which has for long been discredited on the Continent. In France, it was stated in the debates on electoral reform in 1909, for 20 years, under second ballots, only once had a majority outside been represented by a majority inside the Chamber, and the average representation for the two decades had amounted to only 45 per cent. of the voters. Writing to me after the New Zealand elections in 1909, the Hon. George Fowlds (Minister of Education), who has long supported effective voting, said, "The only result of the second ballot system in New Zealand has been to strengthen the movement in favour of proportional representation." And Mr. Paul, a Labour member in the Dominion, is making every effort to have effective voting included in the platform of the New Zealand Labour Party. Further encouragement to continue our work came when Belgium adopted the principle of proportional representation in 1898.

The closing year of the century found the Effective Voting League in the thick of its first election campaign. There is little doubt that the best time for advancing a political reform is during an election, and it was interesting to note how many candidates came to our support. We had an interesting meeting at Parliament House for members just about that time. An opponent of the reform, who was present, complained that we were late in beginning our meeting. "We always begin punctually under the present system," he remarked. "Yes," some one replied, "but we always finish so badly." "Oh, I always finish well enough," was the pert rejoinder; "I generally come out on top." "Ah," retorted the other, "I was thinking of the electors." But the doubter did not come out on top at a subsequent election, and his defeat was probably the means of his discovering defects in the old system that no number of successes would have led him into acknowledging. From the two or three members who had supported Mr. Glynn in the previous Parliament we increased our advocates in the Assembly during the campaign to 14. The agitation had been very persistent among the electors, and their approval of the reform was reflected in the minds of their representatives. We inaugurated during that year the series of citizens' meetings convened by the Mayors of the city and suburbs, which has been so successful a feature of our long campaign for electoral justice, and at the present time very few of the mayoral chairs are occupied by men who are not keen supporters of effective voting.

The Hon. Theodore Bruce's connection with the reform dates from that year, when he presided at a meeting in the Adelaide Town Hall during the temporary absence of the Mayor. A consistent supporter of effective voting from that time, it was only natural that when in May, 1909, the candidature of Mr. Bruce (who was then and is now a Vice-President of the league). for a seat in the Legislative Council, gave us an opportunity for working for his return, against a candidate who had stated that he was not satisfied with the working of the system of effective voting, we availed ourselves of it. So much has been written and said about the attitude of the league with regard to Parliamentary candidates that, as its President, I feel that I ought to take this opportunity of stating our reasons for that attitude. From its inception the league has declined to recognise parties in a contest at all. Its sole concern has been, and must be to support effective voters, to whatever party they may belong. To secure the just representation of the whole electorate of whatever size, is the work of the Effective Voting League, and, whatever the individual opinions of the members may be, as an official body they cannot help any candidate who opposes the reform for which they stand.

I remember meeting at a political meeting during a subsequent general election a lady whom I had known as an almost rabid Kingstonian. But the party had failed to find a position for her son in the Civil Service, although their own sons were in that way satisfactorily provided for. So she had thrown in her lot with the other side, which at the time happened to gain a few seats, and the lady was quite sure that her influence had won the day for her former opponents. Leaning forward to whisper as if her next remark were too delicate for the ears of a gentleman sitting near, she said, "Do you know, I don't believe the Premier has any backbone!" I laughed, and said that I thought most people held the same belief. To my amusement and astonishment she then asked quite seriously, "Do you think that is why he stoops so much?" There was no doubt in her mind that the missing back bone had reference to the physical and not to the moral malformation of the gentleman in question.

CHAPTER XXII
A VISIT TO NEW SOUTH WALES

Early in the year 1900 the Hon. B. R. Wise, then Attorney-General of New South Wales, suggested a campaign for effective voting in the mother State, with the object of educating the people, so that effective voting might be applied for the first Federal elections. Mrs. Young and I left Adelaide on May 10 of that year to inaugurate the movement in New South Wales. During the few hours spent in Melbourne Professor Nanson, the Victorian leader of the reform, with another earnest worker (Mr. Bowditch), called on us, and we had a pleasant talk over the proposed campaign. The power of The Age had already been felt, when, at the convention election, the 10 successful candidates were nominees of that paper, and at that time it was a sturdy opponent of proportional representation. The Argus, on the other hand, had done yeoman service in the advocacy of the reform from the time that Tasmania had so successfully experimented with the system. As we were going straight through to Sydney, we were able only to suggest arrangements for a possible campaign on our return. Our Sydney visit lasted eight weeks, during which time we addressed between 20 and 30 public meetings. Our welcome to the harbour city was most enthusiastic, and our first meeting, held in the Protestant Hall, on the Wednesday after our arrival, with the Attorney-General in the chair, was packed. The greatest interest was shown in the counting of the 387 votes taken at the meeting. Miss Rose Scott, however, had paved the way for the successful public meeting by a reception at her house on the previous Monday, at which we met Mr. Wise, Sir William McMillan, Mr. (afterwards Sr. Walker), Mr. (now Sir A. J.) Gould, Mr. Bruce Smith, Mr. W. Holman, and several other prominent citizens. The reform was taken up earnestly by most of these gentlemen. Sir William McMillan was appointed the first President of the league, which was formed before we left Sydney. During the first week of our visit we dined with Dr. and Mrs. Garran, who, with their son (Mr. Robert Garran, C.M.G., afterwards the collaborateur of Sir John Quick in the compilation of the "Annotated Constitution of the Australian Commonwealth"), were keen supporters of effective voting. Among the host of well-known people who came after dinner to meet us was Mr. (now Sir) George Reid, with whom we had an interesting talk over the much-discussed "Yes-No" Policy. We had both opposed the Bill on its first appeal to the people, and seized the occasion to thank Mr. Reid for his share in delaying the measure. "You think the Bill as amended an improvement?" he asked. "Probably," replied Mrs. Young, "but as I didn't think the improvement great enough, I voted against it both times." But I had not done so, and my vote on the second occasion was in favour of the Bill.

But, as Mr. Reid admitted, the dislike of most reformers for federation was natural enough, for it was only to be expected that "reforms would be difficult to get with such a huge, unwieldy mass" to be moved before they could be won. And experience has proved the correctness of the view expressed. Anything in the nature of a real reform, judging from the experience of the past, will take a long time to bring about. I am convinced that had not South Australia already adopted the principle of the all-round land tax, the progressive form would have been the only one suggested or heard of from either party. Politicians are so apt to take the line of least resistance, and when thousands of votes of small landowners are to be won through the advocacy of an exemption, exemptions there will be. The whole system of taxation is wrong, it seems to me, and though, as a matter of expediency, sometimes from conviction, many people advocate the opposite course, I have long felt that taxation should not be imposed according to the ability to pay so much as according to benefits received from the State. We are frequently warned against expecting too much from Federation during its earlier stages, but experience teaches us that, as with human beings, so with nations, a wrong or a right beginning is responsible to a great extent for right or wrong development. I have the strongest hopes for the future of Australia, but the people must never be allowed to forget that eternal vigilance, as in the past, must still in the future be the price we must pay for our liberty. Later, Mr. Reid presided at our Parliament House meeting, and afterwards entertained us at afternoon tea. But one of our pleasantest memories was of a day spent with the great freetrader and Mrs. Reid at their Strathfield home. I was anxious to hear Mr. Reid speak, and was glad when the opportunity arose on the occasion of a no-confidence debate. But he was by no means at his best, and it was not until I heard him in his famous freetrade speech on his first visit to Adelaide that I realized how great an orator he was. At the close of the no-confidence debate the triumphant remark of an admirer that "Adelaide couldn't produce a speaker like that" showed me that a prophet sometimes hath honour, even in his own country.

Mr. Wise was a brilliant speaker, and a most cultured man, and a delightful talker. Of Mrs. Parkes, then President of the Women's Liberal League, I saw much. She was a fine speaker, and a very clear-headed thinker. Her organizing faculty was remarkable, and her death a year or two ago was a distinct loss to her party. Her home life was a standing example of the fallacy of the old idea that a woman who takes up public work must necessarily neglect her family. Mrs. Barbara Baynton was a woman of a quite different type, clever and emotional, as one would expect the author of the brilliant but tragic "Bush Studies" to be. She was strongly opposed to Federation, as, indeed were large numbers of clever people in New South Wales. Frank Fox (afterwards connected with The Lone Hand), Bertram Stevens (author of "An Anthology of Australian Verse"), Judge Backhouse (who was probably the only Socialist Judge on the Australian Bench), were frequent visitors at Miss Scott's, and were all interesting people. An afternoon meeting on effective voting was arranged at the Sydney University, I think, by Dr. Anderson Stuart. We were charmed with the university and its beautiful surroundings. Among the visitors that afternoon was Mrs. David, a charming and well-read woman, whose book describing an expedition to Funafuti, is delightful. We afterwards dined with her and Professor David, and spent a pleasant hour with them.

I was not neglectful of other reforms while on this campaign, and found time to interest myself in the State children's work with which my friend, Mrs. Garran, was so intimately connected. We went to Liverpool one day to visit the benevolent institution for men. There were some hundreds of men there housed in a huge building reminiscent of the early convict days. If not the whole, parts of it had been built by the convicts, and the massive stone staircase suggested to our minds the horrors of convict settlement. I have always resented the injury done to this new country by the foundation of penal settlements, through which Botany Bay lost its natural connotation as a habitat for wonderful flora, and became known only as a place where convicts were sent for three-quarters of a century. Barrington's couplet, written as a prologue at the opening of the Playhouse, Sydney, in 1796, to a play given by convicts—

True patriots we, for be it understood

We left our country for our country's good—

was clever, but untrue. All experience proves that while it is a terrible injury to a new country to be settled by convicts, it is a real injury also to the people from whom they are sent, to shovel out of sight all their failures, and neither try to lessen their numbers nor to reclaim them to orderly civil life. It was not till Australia refused any longer to receive convicts, as Virginia had previously done, that serious efforts were made to amend the criminal code of England, or to use reformatory methods first with young and afterwards with older offenders. Another pleasant trip was one we took to Parramatta. The Government launch was courteously placed at our disposal to visit the Parramatta Home for Women, where also we found some comfortable homes for old couples. The separation of old people who would prefer to spend the last years of their life together is I consider, an outrage on society. One of my chief desires has been to establish such homes for destitute couples in South Australia, and to every woman who may be appointed as a member of the Destitute Board in future I appeal to do her utmost to change our methods of treatment with regard to old couples, so that to the curse of poverty may not be added the cruelty of enforced separation. Women in New South Wales were striving for the franchise at that time, and we had the pleasure of speaking at one of their big meetings. And what fine public meetings they had in Sydney! People there seemed to take a greater interest in politics than here, and crowded attendances were frequent at political meetings, even when there was no election to stir them up. It was a Sydney lady who produced this amusing Limerick in my honour:—

> There was a Grand Dame of Australia
>
> Who proved the block system a failure.
>
> She taught creatures in coats
>
> What to do with their votes,
>
> This Effective Grand Dame of Australia!

The third line will perhaps preclude the necessity for pointing out that the author was an ardent suffragist! To an enlightened woman also was probably due the retort to a gentleman's statement that "Miss Spence was a good man lost," that, "On the contrary she thought she was a good woman saved." "In what way?" he asked. "Saved for the benefit of her country, instead of having her energies restricted to the advantages of one home," was the reply. And for this I have sometimes felt very thankful myself that I have been free to devote what gifts I possess to what I consider best for the advantage and the uplifting of humanity. Before leaving Sydney I tried once more to find a publisher for "Gathered In," but was assured that the only novels worth publishing in Australia were sporting or political novels.

I was in my seventy-fifth year at the time of this visit, but the joy of being enabled to extend the influence of our reform to other States was so great that the years rolled back and left me as full of life and vigour and zeal as I had ever been. Our work had by no means been confined to the city and suburbs, as we spoke at a few country towns as well. At Albury, where we stopped on our way back to Victoria, we were greeted by a crowded and enthusiastic audience in the fine hall of the Mechanics' Institute. We had passed through a snowstorm just before reaching Albury, and the country was very beautiful in the afternoon, when our friends drove us through the district. The Murray was in flood, and the "water, water everywhere" sparkling in the winter sunshine, with the snowcapped Australian Alps in the background, made an exquisite picture. Albury was the only town we visited in our travels which still retained the old custom of the town crier.

Sitting in the room of the hotel after dinner, we were startled at hearing our names and our mission proclaimed to the world at large, to the accompaniment t of a clanging bell and introduced by the old-fashioned formula, "Oyez! oyez! oyez!" Our work in Victoria was limited, but included a delightful trip to Castlemaine. We were impressed with the fine Mechanics' Hall of that town, in which we spoke to a large audience. But a few years later the splendid building, with many others in the town, was razed to the ground by a disastrous cyclone. Returning from Castlemaine, we had an amusing experience in the train. I had laid aside my knitting, which is the usual companion of my travels, to teach Mrs. Young the game of "Patience," but at one of the stations a foreign gentleman entered the carriage, when we immediately put aside the cards. After chatting awhile, he expressed regret that he had been the cause of the banishment of our cards, and "Would the ladies not kindly tell him his fortune also?" He was as much amused as we were when we explained that we were reformers and not fortune tellers. I have been a great lover of card games all my life; patience in solitude, and cribbage, whist, and bridge have been the almost invariable accompaniments of my evenings spent at home or with my friends. Reading and knitting were often indulged in, but patience was a change and a rest and relief to the mind. I have always had the idea that card games are an excellent incentive to the memory. We had an afternoon meeting in the Melbourne Town Hall to inaugurate a league in Victoria, at which Dr. Barrett, the Rev. Dr. Bevan, Professor Nanson, and I were the principal speakers. Just recently I wrote to the Victorian Minister who had charge of the Preferential Voting Bill in the Victorian Parliament to ask him to consider the merits of effective voting; but, like most other politicians, the Minister did not find the time opportune for considering the question of electoral justice for all parties. I remained in Victoria to spend a month with my family and friends after Mrs. Young returned to Adelaide. The death of my dear brother John, whose sympathy and help had always meant so much to me, shortly after my return, followed by that of my brother William in New Zealand, left me the sole survivor of the generation which had sailed from Scotland in 1839.

CHAPTER XXIII
MORE PUBLIC WORK

For the co-operative movement I had always felt the keenest sympathy. I saw in it the liberation of the small wage-earner from the toils of the middlemen. I thought moreover that the incentive to thrift so strongly encouraged by co-operative societies would be a tremendous gain to the community as well as to the individual. How many people owe a comfortable old age to the delight of seeing their first small profits in a co-operative concern, or their savings in a building society accumulating steadily and surely, if but slowly? And I have always had a disposition to encourage anything that would tend to lighten the burden of the worker. So that when in 1901 Mrs. Agnes Milne placed before me a suggestion for the formation of a women's co-operative clothing factory, I was glad to do what I could to further an extension in South Australia of the movement, which, from its inception in older countries, had made so strong an appeal to my reason. A band of women workers were prepared to associate for the mutual benefit of the operatives in the shirtmaking and clothing trades. Under the title of the South Australian Co-operative Clothing Company, Limited, they proposed to take over and carry on a small private factory, owned by one of themselves, which had found it difficult to compete against large firms working with the latest machinery. I was sure of finding many sympathizers among my friends, and was successful in disposing of a fair number of shares. The movement had already gained support from thinking working women, and by the time we were ready to form ourselves into a company we were hopeful of success. I was appointed, and have since remained the first President of the board of directors; and, unless prevented by illness or absence from the State, I have never failed to be present at all meetings. The introduction of Wages Boards added to the keen competition between merchants, had made the task of carrying on successfully most difficult, but we hoped that as the idea gained publicity we should benefit proportionately. It was a great blow to us, when at the close of the first year we were able to declare a dividend of 1/ a share, the merchants closed down upon us and reduced their payments by 6d. or 9d. per dozen. But in spite of drawbacks we have maintained the struggle successfully, though sometimes at disheartening cost to the workers and officials of the society. I feel, however, that the reward of success due to this plucky band of women workers will come in the near future, for at no other time probably has the position looked more hopeful than during the present year.

During this same year the Effective Voting League made a new departure in its propaganda work by inviting Sir Edward Braddon to address a meeting in the Adelaide Town Hall. As Premier of Tasmania, Sir Edward had inaugurated the reform in the gallant little island State, and he was able to speak with authority on the practicability and the justice of effective voting. His visit was followed a year later by one from Sr. Keating, another enthusiastic Tasmanian supporter, whose lecture inspired South Australian workers to even greater efforts, and carried conviction to the minds of many waverers. At that meeting we first introduced the successful method of explanation by means of limelight slides. The idea of explaining the whole system by pictures had seemed impossible, but every step of the counting can be shown so simply and clearly by this means as to make an understanding of the system a certainty. To the majority of people an appeal to reason and understanding is made much more easily through the eye than through the ear. The year 1902 saw an advance in the Parliamentary agitation of the reform, when the Hon. Joseph (now Senator) Vardon introduced a Bill for the first time into the Legislative Council. The measure had been excellently prepared by Mr. J. H. Vaughan, LL.B., with the assistance of the members of the executive of the Effective Voting League, among whom were Messrs. Crawford Vaughan and E. A. Anstey. The Bill sought to apply effective voting to existing electoral districts, which, though not nearly so satisfactory as larger districts, nevertheless made the application of effective voting possible. With the enlargement of the district on the alteration of the Constitution subsequent to federation becoming an accomplished fact, the league was unanimous in its desire to seek the line of least resistance by avoiding a change in the Constitution that an alteration in electoral boundaries would have necessitated.

To Mr. Vardon, when he was a candidate for Legislative honours in 1900 the usual questions were sent from the league; but, as he had not studied the question he declined to pledge himself to support the reform. Realizing, however, the necessity of enquiring into all public matters, he decided to study the Hare system, but the league declined to support him without a written pledge. Still he was elected, and immediately afterwards studied effective voting, became convinced of its justice, and has remained a devoted advocate. Our experience with legislators had usually been of the opposite nature. Pledged adherents to effective voting during an election campaign, as members they no longer saw the necessity for a change in a method of voting which had placed them safely in Parliament; but in Mr. Vardon we found a man whose conversion to effective voting was a matter of principle, and not a question of gathering votes. That was why the league selected him as its Parliamentary advocate when effective voting first took definite shape in the form of a Bill. When, later, Mr. E. H. Coombe, M.P., took charge of the Bill in the Assembly although the growth in public opinion in favour of effective voting had been surprising, the coalition between the Liberal and Labour parties strengthened their combined position and weakened the allegiance of their elected members to a reform which would probably affect their vested interests in the Legislature. Mr. Coombe had not been an easy convert to proportional representation. He had attended my first lecture at Gawler, but saw difficulties in the way of accepting the Hare system as propounded by me. His experiments were interesting. Assuming a constituency of 100 electors with 10 members, he filled in 60 Conservative and 40 Liberal voting papers. The proportion of members to each party should be six Conservatives and four Liberals, and when he found that by no amount of manipulation could this result be altered he became a convert to effective voting. His able advocacy of the reform is too well known to need further reference; but I should like now to thank those members, including Mr. K. W. Duncan, who have in turn led the crusade for righteous representation in both Houses of Parliament, for of them may it truly be said that the interests of the people as a whole were their first consideration. Before I left for America I saw the growing power and strength of the Labour Party. I rejoiced that a new star had arisen in the political firmament. I looked to it as a party that would support every cause that tended towards righteousness. I expected it, as a reform party, to take up effective voting, because effective voting was a reform. I hoped that a party whose motto was "Trust the people" would have adopted a reform by means of which alone it would be possible for the people to gain control over its Legislature and its Government. Alas! for human hopes that depend on parties for their realization! As time after time I have seen defections from the ranks of proportionalists, and people have said to me:—"Give it up, Miss Spence. Why trouble longer? Human nature is too bad," I have answered, "No; these politicians are but the ephemeral creations of a day or a month, or a year; this reform is for all time, and must prevail, and I will never give it up."

During my many visits to Melbourne and Sydney I had been much impressed with the influence and the power for good of the local branches of the world-famed National Council of Women. I had long hoped for the establishment of a branch in South Australia, and was delighted to fall in with a suggestion made by the Countess of Aberdeen (Vice-President-at-large of the International Council), through Lady Cockburn, that a council should be formed in South Australia. The inaugural meeting in September, 1902, was splendidly attended, and it was on a resolution moved by me that the council came into existence. Lady Way was the first President, and I was one of the Vice-Presidents. I gave several addresses, and in 1904 contributed a paper on "Epileptics." In dealing with this subject I owed much to the splendid help I received from my dear friend Miss Alice Henry, of Victoria, now in Chicago, whose writings on epileptics and weak-minded children have contributed largely to the awakening of the public conscience to a sense of duty towards these social weaklings. In 1905 I contributed a paper to the quinquennial meeting of the International Council of Women, held at Berlin, on the laws relating to women and children in

South Australia, and gave an account of the philanthropic institutions of the State, with special reference to the State Children's Council and Juvenile Courts. The work of the National Council in this State was disappointing to many earnest women, who had hoped to find in it a means for the social, political, and philanthropic education of the women of South Australia. Had the council been formed before we had obtained the vote there would probably have been more cohesion and a greater sustained effort to make it a useful body. But as it was there was so apparent a disinclination to touch "live" subjects that interest in the meetings dwindled, and in 1906 I resigned my position on the executive in order to have more time to spare for other public work.

A problem which was occasioning the State Children's Council much anxious thought was how to deal effectively with the ever-increasing number of the "children of the streets". Boys and girls alike, who should either be at school or engaged at some useful occupation, were roaming the streets and parks, uncontrolled and sometimes uncontrollable. We recognised that their condition was one of moral peril, and graduation to criminality from these nurseries of crime so frequently occurred that State interference seemed absolutely imperative to save the neglected unfortunates for a worthier citizenship. It is much easier and far more economical to save the child than to punish the criminal. One of the most effective means of clearing the streets would be to raise the compulsory age for school attendance up to the time of employment. That truancy was to a great extent responsible for these juvenile delinquents was proved by the fact that more then one-half of the lads sent to Magill had committed the crimes for which they were first convicted while truanting. Moreover, an improvement was noticed immediately on the amendment of the compulsory attendance clauses in the Education Act. Truancy—the wicket gate of the road to ruin in youth—should be barred as effectively as possible, and the best way to bar it is to make every day a compulsory school day, unless the excuse for absence be abundantly sufficient. Another aspect of the neglected children problem, which Federal action alone will solve, is in dealing with cases of neglect by desertion. At present each State is put to great trouble and expense through defaulting parents. Federal legislation would render it possible to have an order for payment made in one State collected and remitted by an officer in another State. By this means thousands of pounds a year could be saved to the various States, and many a child prevented from becoming a burden to the people at large. These are some of the problems awaiting solution and the women of South Australia will do well to make the salvation of these neglected waifs a personal care and responsibility. Perhaps no other work of the State Children's Council has more practically shown their appreciation of the capabilities of the children under their care than the establishment of the State children's advancement fund. This is to enable State children who show any aptitude, to pursue their education through the continuation schools to the University. To private subscriptions for this purpose the Government have added a subsidy of 50 pounds, and already some children are availing themselves of this splendid opportunity to rise in the world. The longer I live the prouder I feel that I have been enabled to assist in this splendid work for the benefit of humanity.

The years as they passed left me with wider interests in, deeper sympathies with, and greater knowledge of the world and its people. Each year found "one thing worth beginning, one thread of life worth spinning." The pleasure I derived from the more extended intellectual activity of my later years was due largely to my association with a band of cultured and earnest women interested in social, political, and other public questions—women who, seeing "the tides of things," desired so to direct them that each wave of progress should carry the people to a higher place on the sands of life. To the outside world little is known of the beginnings and endings of social movements, which, taken separately, perhaps appear of small consequence, but which in the aggregate count for a great deal in what is popularly known as the forward movement. To such as these belonged an interesting association of women, which, meeting at first informally, grew eventually into a useful organization for the intellectual and moral development of those who were fortunate enough to be associated with it. This was the "Social Students' Society," of which Miss A. L. Tomkinson was the secretary and I the first President. One of the addresses I gave was on "Education," and among others whose addresses helped us considerably was the Director of Education (Mr. A. Williams). Speakers from all parties addressed the association, and while the society existed a good deal of educational work was done. Much interest was taken in the question of public playgrounds for children, and we succeeded in interesting the City Council in the movement; but, owing to lack of funds, the scheme for the time being was left in abeyance.

In the agitation for the public ownership of the tramways, I was glad to take a share. The private ownership of monopolies is indefensible, and my American experiences of the injustice of the system strengthened my resolve to do my utmost to prevent the growth of the evil in South Australia. My attitude on the question alienated a number of friends, both from me personally and from effective voting, so intolerant had people become of any opposition to their own opinions. The result of the referendum was disappointing, and, I shall always consider, a grave reflection on a democratic community which permits a referendum to be taken under a system of plural voting which makes the whole proceeding a farce. But the citizens of Adelaide have need to be grateful to the patriotic zeal of those who, led by the late Cornelius Proud fought for the public ownership of the tramways.

These years of activity were crossed by sickness and sorrow. For the first time in a long life, which had already extended almost a decade beyond the allotted span, I became seriously ill. To be thus laid low by sickness was a deep affliction to one of my active temperament; but, if sickness brings trouble, it often brings joy in the tender care and appreciation of hosts of friends, and this joy I realized to the fullest extent. The following year (1904) was darkened by the tragic death of my ward, and once more my home was broken up, and with Miss Gregory I went to live with my good friends Mr. and Mrs. Quilty, in North Norwood. From then on my life has flowed easily and pleasantly, marred only by the sadness of farewells of many old friends and comrades on my life's journey, who one by one have passed "through Nature to eternity."

Much as I have written during the past 40 years, it was reserved for my old age to discover within me the power of poetical expression. I had rhymed in my youth and translated French verse, but until I wrote my one sonnet, poetry had been an untried field. The one-sided pessimistic pictures that Australian poets and writers present are false in the impression they make on the outside world and on ourselves. They lead us to forget the beauty and the brightness of the world we live in. What we need is, as Matthew Arnold says of life, "to see Australia steadily and see it whole." It is not wise to allow the "deadbeat"—the remittance man, the gaunt shepherd with his starving flocks and herds, the free selector on an arid patch, the drink shanty where the rouseabouts and shearers knock down their cheques, the race meeting where high and low, rich and poor, are filled with the gambler's ill luck—fill the foreground of the picture of Australian life. These reflections led me to a protest, in the form of a sonnet published in The Register some years ago:—

> When will some new Australian poet rise
>
> To all the height and glory of his theme?
>
> Nor on the sombre side for ever dream
>
> Our hare, baked plains, our pitiless blue skies,
>
> 'Neath which the haggard bushman strains his eyes
>
> To find some waterhole or hidden stream
>
> To save himself and flocks in want extreme!
>
> This is not all Australia! Let us prize
>
> Our grand inheritance! Had sunny Greece
>
> More light, more glow, more freedom, or more mirth?
>
> Ours are wide vistas bathed in purest air—
>
> Youth's outdoor pleasures, Age's indoor peace—
>
> Where could we find a fairer home on earth
>
> Which we ourselves are free to make more fair?

Just as years before my interest had been kindled in the establishment of our system of State education, and later in the University and higher education, so more recently has the inauguration of the Froebel system of kindergarten training appealed most strongly to my reason and judgment. There was a time in the history of education, long after the necessity for expert teaching in primary and secondary schools had been recognised, when the training of the infant mind was left to the least skilled assistant on the staff of a school. With the late Mr. J. A. Hartley, whose theory was that the earliest beginnings of education needed even greater skill in the teacher than the higher branches, I had long regarded the policy as mistaken; but modern educationists have changed all that, and the training of tiny mites of two or three summers and upwards is regarded as of equal importance with that of children of a larger growth. South Australia owes its free kindergarten to the personal initiative and private munificence of the Rev. Bertram Hawker, youngest son of the late Hon. G. C. Hawker. I had already met, and admired the kindergarten work of, Miss Newton when in Sydney, and was delighted when she accepted Mr. Hawker's invitation to inaugurate the system in Adelaide. Indeed, the time of her stay here during September, 1905, might well have been regarded as a special visitation of educational experts, for, in addition to Miss Newton, the directors of education from New South Wales and Victoria (Messrs. G. H. Knibbs and F. Tate) took part in the celebrations. Many interesting meetings led up to the formation of the Kindergarten Union. My niece, Mrs. J. P. Morice, was appointed hon. secretary, and I became one of the Vice-Presidents. On joining the union I was proud of the fact that I was the first member to pay a subscription. The free kindergarten has come to South Australia to stay, and is fast growing into an integral part of our system of education. I have rejoiced in the progress of the movement, and feel that the future will witness the realization of my ideal of a ladder that will reach from the kindergarten to the University, as outlined in articles I wrote for The Register at that time.

CHAPTER XXIV
THE EIGHTIETH MILESTONE AND THE END

On October 31, 1905, I celebrated my eightieth birthday. Twelve months earlier, writing to a friend, I said:—"I entered my eightieth year on Monday, and I enjoy life as much as I did at 18; indeed, in many respects I enjoy it more." The birthday gathering took place in the schoolroom of the Unitarian Church, the church to which I had owed so much happiness through the lifting of the dark shadows of my earlier religious beliefs. Surrounded by friends who had taken their share in the development of my beloved State, I realized one of the happiest times of my life. I had hoped that the celebration would have helped the cause of effective voting, which had been predominant in my mind since 1859. By my interests and work in so many other directions—in literature, journalism, education, philanthropy, and religion—which had been testified to by so many notable people on that occasion, I hoped to prove that I was not a mere faddist, who could be led away by a chimerical fantasy. I wanted the world to understand that I was a clear-brained, commonsense woman of the world, whose views on effective voting and other political questions were as worthy of credence as her work in other directions had been worthy of acceptance. The greetings of my many friends from all parts of the Commonwealth on that day brought so much joy to me that there was little wonder I was able to conclude my birthday poem "Australian spring" with the lines:—

With eighty winters o'er my head,

Within my heart there's Spring.

Full as my life was with its immediate interests, the growth and development of the outside world claimed a good share of my attention. The heated controversies in the motherland over the preachings and teaching of the Rev. R. J. Campbell found their echo here, and I was glad to be able to support in pulpit and newspaper the stand made by t he courageous London preacher of modern thought. How changed the outlook of the world from my childhood's days, when Sunday was a day of strict theological habit, from which no departure could be permitted! The laxity of modern life, by comparison is, I think, somewhat appalling. We have made the mistake of breaking away from old beliefs and convictions without replacing them with something better. We do not make as much, or as good, use of our Sundays as we might do. There is a medium between the rigid Sabbatarianism of our ancestors and the absolute waste of the day of rest in mere pleasure and frivolity. All the world is deploring the secularizing of Sunday. Not only is churchgoing perfunctory or absent, but in all ranks of life there is a disposition to make it a day of rest and amusement—sometimes the amusement rather than the rest. Sunday, the Sabbath, as Alex McLaren pointed out to me, is not a day taken from us, but a day given to us. "Behold, I have given you the Sabbath!" For what? For rest for man and beast, but also to be a milestone in our upward and onward progress—a day for not only wearing best clothes, but for reading our best books and thinking our best thoughts. I have often grieved at the small congregations in other churches no less than in my own, and the grief was aggravated by the knowledge that those who were absent from church were not necessarily otherwise well employed. I derived so much pleasure from the excellent and cultured sermons of my friend the Rev. John Reid during his term of office here that I regretted the fact that others who might gain equally from them were not there to hear them. I would like to see among the young people a finer conception of the duties of citizenship, which, if not finding expression in church attendance, may develop in some way that will be noble and useful to society.

In the meantime the work of the Effective Voting League had been rather at a standstill. Mrs. Young's illness had caused her resignation, and until she again took up the work nothing further was done to help Mr. Coombe in his Parliamentary agitation. In 1908, however, we began a vigorous campaign, and towards the close of the year the propaganda work was being carried into all parts of the State. Although I was then 83, I travelled to Petersburg to lecture to a good audience. On the same night Mrs. Young addressed a fine gathering at Mount Gambier, and from that time the work has gone on unceasingly. The last great effort was made through the newspaper ballot of September, 1909, when a public count of about 10,000 votes was completed with all explanations during the evening. The difficulties that were supposed to stand in the way of a general acceptance of effective voting have been entirely swept away. Tasmania and South Africa have successfully demonstrated the practicability, no less than the justice, of the system. Now we get to the bedrock of the objections raised to its adoption, and we find that they exist only in the minds of the politicians themselves; but the people have faith in effective voting, and I believe the time to be near when they will demand equitable representation in every Legislature in the world. The movement has gone too far to be checked, and the electoral unrest which is so common all over the world will eventually find expression in the best of all electoral systems, which I claim to be effective voting.

Among the many friends I had made in the other States there was none I admired more for her public spiritedness than Miss Vida Goldstein. I have been associated with her on many platforms and in many branches of work. Her versatility is great, but there is little doubt that her chief work lies in helping women and children. Her life is practically spent in battling for her sex. Although I was the first woman in Australia to become a Parliamentary candidate, Miss Goldstein has since exceeded my achievement by a second candidature for the Senate. It was during her visit here last May-June as a delegate to the State Children's Congress that she inaugurated the Women's Non-party Political Association, which is apparently a growing force. In a general way the aims of the society bear a strong resemblance to those of the social students' society, many of its members having also belonged to the earlier association. It was a hopeful sign to me that it included among its members people of all political views working chiefly in the interests of women and children. Of this Society also I became the first President, and the fact that on its platform was included proportional representation was an incentive for me to work for it. The education of women on public and social questions, so that they will be able to work side by side with the opposite sex for the public good will, I think, help in the solution of social problems that are now obstacles in the path of progress. In addition to other literary work for the year 1909 I was asked by Miss Alice Henry to revise my book on State children in order to make it acceptable and applicable to American conditions. It was a big undertaking, but I think successful. The book, as originally written had already done good work in Western Australia, where the conditions of infant mortality were extremely alarming, and in England also; and there is ample scope for such a work in America, which is still far behind even the most backward Australian State in its care for dependent children.

As a President of three societies, a Vice-President of two others, a member of two of the most important boards in the State for the care of the destitute, the deserted, and the dependent, with a correspondence that touches on many parts of the Empire, and two continents besides, with my faculty for the appreciation of good literature still unimpaired, with my domestic interests so dear to me, and my constant knitting for the infants under the care of the State Inspector—I find my life as an octogenarian more varied in its occupations and interests than ever before. Looking back from the progressive heights of 1910 through the long vista of years, numbering upwards of four-fifths of a century, I rejoice at the progress the world has made. Side by side with the development of my State my life has slowly unfolded itself. My connection with many of the reforms to which is due this development has been intimate, and (I think I am justified in saying) oftentimes helpful. While other States of the Commonwealth and the Dominion of New Zealand have made remarkable progress, none has eclipsed the rapid growth of the State to which the steps of my family were directed in 1839. Its growth has been more remarkable, because it has been primarily due to its initiation of many social and political reforms which have since been adopted by other and older countries. "Australia, lead us further," is the cry of reformers in America. We have led in so many things, and though America may claim the honour of being the birthplace of the more modern theory of land values taxation, I rejoice that South Australia was the first country in the world with the courage and the foresight to adopt the tax on land values without exemption. That she is still lagging behind

Tasmania and South Africa in the adoption of effective voting, as the only scientific system of electoral reform, is the sorrow of my old age. The fact that South Australia has been the happy hunting ground of the faddist has frequently been urged as a reproach against this State. Its more patriotic citizens will rejoice in the truth of the statement, and their prayer will probably be that not fewer but more advanced thinkers will arise to carry this glorious inheritance beneath the Southern Cross to higher and nobler heights of physical and human development than civilization has yet dreamed of or achieved. The Utopia of yesterday is the possession of today, and opens the way to the Utopia of tomorrow. The haunting horror of older civilizations—divorcing the people from their natural inheritance in the soil, and filling the towns with myriads of human souls dragged down by poverty, misery, and crime—is already casting its shadow over the future of Australia; but there is hope in the fact that a new generation has arisen untrammelled by tradition, which, having the experience of older countries before it, and benefiting from the advantages of the freer life and the greater opportunities afforded by a new country, gives promise of ultimately finding the solution of the hitherto unsolved problem of making country life as attractive to the masses as that of the towns and cities. As time goes on the effect of education must tell, and the generations that are to come will be more enlightened and more altruistic, and the tendency of the world will be more and more, even as it is now, towards higher and nobler conceptions of human happiness. I have lived through a glorious age of progress. Born in "the wonderful century," I have watched the growth of the movement for the uplifting of the masses, from the Reform Bill of 1832 to the demands for adult suffrage. As a member of a church which allows women to speak in the pulpit, a citizen of a State which gives womanhood a vote for the Assembly, a citizen of a Commonwealth which fully enfranchises me for both Senate and Representatives, and a member of a community which was foremost in conferring University degrees on women, I have benefited from the advancement of the educational and political status of women for which the Victorian era will probably stand unrivalled in the annals of the world's history. I have lived through the period of repressed childhood, and witnessed the dawn of a new era which has made the dwellers in youth's "golden age" the most important factor in human development. I have watched the growth of Adelaide from the condition of a scattered hamlet to that of one of the finest cities in the southern hemisphere; I have seen the evolution of South Australia from a province to an important State in a great Commonwealth. All through my life I have tried to live up to the best that was in me, and I should like to be remembered as one who never swerved in her efforts to do her duty alike to herself and her fellow-citizens. Mistakes I have made, as all are liable to do, but I have done my best. And when life has closed for me, let those who knew me best speak and think of me as One who never turned her back, but marched breast forward,

> Never doubted clouds would break,
>
> Never dreamed, though right were worsted, wrong would triumph,
>
> Held we fall to rise, are baffled to fight better,
>
> Sleep to wake.
>
> No nobler epitaph would I desire.

Printed in Great Britain
by Amazon